D1373307

m. 824=
660/-

ANNE WILLAN'S
LOOK & COOK
Main Dish Vegetables

660/-

ANNE WILLAN'S
LOOK & COOK

Main Dish Vegetables

DORLING KINDERSLEY
LONDON • NEW YORK • STUTTGART

BOOK BEAUTY
191, Dhaka New Market
Dhaka-5. Ph:-507519

A DORLING KINDERSLEY BOOK

Created and Produced by
CARROLL & BROWN LIMITED
5 Lonsdale Road
London NW6 6RA

Editorial Director Jeni Wright
Editors Jennifer Feller
Norma MacMillan
Sally Poole
Stella Vayne

Art Editor Vicky Zentner
Designers Lucy De Rosa
Lyndel Donaldson
Wendy Rogers
Mary Staples
Lisa Webb

First published in Great Britain in 1992
by Dorling Kindersley Limited
9 Henrietta Street, London WC2E 8PS

Copyright © 1992 Dorling Kindersley Limited
Text copyright © 1992 Anne Willan Inc.

All rights reserved. No part of this publication may be
reproduced, stored in a retrieval system, or transmitted in
any form or by any means, electronic, mechanical, photocopying,
recording or otherwise, without the prior written permission
of the copyright owner.
A CIP catalogue record for this book is available
from the British Library
ISBN 0-86318-988-1

Reproduced by Colourscan, Singapore
Printed and bound in Italy by A. Mondadori, Verona

CONTENTS

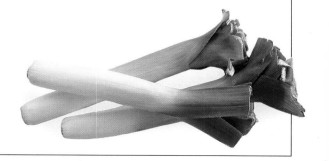

VEGETABLES

THE LOOK & COOK APPROACH

Welcome to **Main Dish Vegetables,** and the *Look & Cook* series. These volumes are designed to be the simplest, most informative cookbooks you'll ever own. They are the closest I can come to sharing my techniques for cooking my favourite recipes without actually being with you in the kitchen looking over your shoulder.

EQUIPMENT

Equipment and ingredients often determine whether or not you can cook a particular dish, so *Look & Cook* illustrates everything you need at the beginning of each recipe. You'll see at a glance how long a recipe takes to cook, how many servings it makes, what the finished dish looks like, and how much preparation can be done ahead. When you start to cook, you'll find the preparation and cooking are organized into easy-to-follow steps. Each stage is colour-coded and everything is shown in photographs with brief text to go with each step. You will never be in doubt about what it is you are doing, why you are doing it, or how it should look.

INGREDIENTS

🍲 SERVES 6-8   🥄 WORK TIME 45-50 MINUTES   🍳 COOKING TIME 25-35 MINUTES

I've also included helpful hints and ideas under "Anne Says". These may list an alternative ingredient or piece of equipment, or sometimes the reason for using a certain method is explained, or there is advice on mastering a particular technique. Similarly, if there is a crucial stage in a recipe when things can go wrong, I've included some warnings called "Take Care".

Many of the photographs are annotated to pinpoint why certain pieces of equipment work best, or how the food should look at that stage of cooking. Because presentation is so important, a picture of the finished dish and serving suggestions are at the end of each recipe.

Thanks to all this information, you can't go wrong. I'll be with you every step of the way. So please, come with me into the kitchen to look, cook, and create some delicious **Main Dish Vegetables.**

WHY VEGETABLES?

Fresh vegetables play a major role in the way we eat today. Modern health concerns have made the combination of high vitamin and low fat content a popular choice at almost every meal. But if that were not enough, the flavour and sweetness of vegetables at their prime is enough reward to enjoy them as main courses in their own right. Whether you choose them stuffed or stir-fried, in a quiche or a stew, you'll find vegetable-based meals to savour all year round.

RECIPE CHOICE

The wide range of recipes given here offers a vegetable-based dish for all occasions and seasons of the year. Choose Calzone or Three-Pepper Pizza with Cheese for a casual supper, Stuffed Vegetable Trio with Walnut-Garlic Sauce for a more elegant dinner. Summer Frittata with Ratatouille makes a delicious and light warm-weather meal, while Mixed Vegetable Curry or Pumpkin Stew can star as hearty meals for colder, winter months.

BREADS AND TARTS

Flemish Vegetable Tart: in this rustic tart, a rich brioche crust holds a generous filling of colourful julienne vegetables in a light custard. *Pissaladière:* the French version of pizza has a Mediterranean topping of onions, herbs, anchovies, olives, and cherry tomatoes. *Three-Pepper Pizza with Cheese:* red, green, and yellow peppers with herbs and mozzarella, make a striking display on a spicy pizza dough. *Three-Pepper Calzone with Cheese:* the pepper filling is wrapped in individual turnovers of pizza dough. *Mushroom and Artichoke Pizzas:* sautéed mushrooms and artichokes moistened with fresh tomato sauce top these cocktail-size pizzas. *Broccoli and Mushroom Quiche:* no main dish vegetable book would be complete without a quiche, the savoury tart from Alsace that has swept the world. *Courgette and Mushroom Quiche:* rounds of courgette, slices of mushroom, and cheese custard are baked in a pastry crust. *Phyllo Pie with Spicy Kale and Sausage:* a savoury combination of kale, onions, and sausage meat fills a flaky phyllo pastry parcel. *Potato and Blue Cheese Phyllo Pie:* thin potato slices layered with blue cheese, bacon, and shallots make a hearty filling for this phyllo pie.

SOUPS AND STEWS

Vegetable Couscous: vegetable-packed version of the traditional North African dish has a highly flavoured broth and skewers of grilled courgette, pepper, and cherry tomatoes. *Vegetable and Lamb Couscous:* herbed lamb cubes are added to the vegetable kebabs, to be served with broth on a bed of couscous. *Fish Couscous:* chunks of monkfish, cooked in a vegetable broth, accompany the couscous. *Genoese Minestrone:* fresh vegetable soup full of red kidney beans, cannellini beans, and macaroni, with a purée of tomato, garlic, and basil stirred in for a burst of fresh flavour. *Soupe au Pistou, Croûtes Gratinées:* French version of minestrone, finished with cheese-topped toasts. *Borscht with Piroshki:* the brilliant red beetroot and cabbage soup is served with little cabbage- and cheese-filled turnovers. *Rustic Borscht:* this version is made with beef shredded into the soup. *Pumpkin Stew:* hearty mixture of courgettes, butternut squash, leeks, tomatoes, celery, turnips, and bacon is served in the pumpkin shell. *Pumpkin Stew with Onion Topping:* fried onion rings and bacon add crunch to savoury pumpkin stew. *Mixed Vegetable Curry:* carrots, potatoes, cauliflower, French beans, and peas are cooked with a fragrant blend of Indian spices and coconut milk. *Winter Vegetable Curry:* curry takes a seasonal turn with winter vegetables cooked in the curry spice mixture.

COLD MAIN DISHES

Mediterranean Vegetable Platter with Garlic Sauce:
a stunning platter of cold cooked
Provençal vegetables is
presented with a zesty
garlic-herb sauce.
*Vegetable Salad
with Tahini
Dressing:* the
same array
of prepared
vegetables is
complemented
by a nutty Middle
Eastern dip made
from tahini (sesame
seed paste), garlic, and
lemon juice. *Mosaic of Vegetables
with Chicken Mousse:* multicoloured layers of carrots,
French beans, and spinach are held in a light chicken
mousse in this terrine, served with piquant mustard sauce.
Mosaic of Vegetables with Cheese: a rich cheese custard binds
layers of colourful vegetables together, and a red pepper
sauce is the accompaniment.

HOT MAIN DISHES

Stuffed Vegetable Trio with Walnut-Garlic Sauce: sweet
onions, courgettes, and ripe tomatoes, with bulghur and
mushroom stuffing, are served with a pungent sauce. *Wild
Rice Stuffed Vegetable Trio:* nutty wild rice and herbs make
the filling for this trio of vegetables. *Vegetable Trio with
Carrot-Rice Stuffing:* vegetables are vivid with grated carrot
in white rice stuffing. *Cabbage with Chestnut and Pork
Stuffing:* cabbage leaves are shaped around an unusual
chestnut stuffing to resemble a whole cabbage. *Baby Green
Cabbages Stuffed with Pork:* pairs of cabbage leaves are filled

with a meaty mixture, shaped into balls, and simmered, to
serve with soured cream. *Gratin of Chicory and Ham:*
braised chicory is wrapped in ham and topped with
béchamel sauce sprinkled with cheese – delicious! *Broccoli
and Cauliflower Gratin:* this vegetarian gratin combines
green and white florets in a cheese sauce.
Individual Gratins of Leek and Ham: pale green
leeks are baked in individual gratins and
decorated with leek julienne. *Artichokes Stuffed
with Mushrooms and Olives:* pungent stuffing
fills globe artichokes, served with red pepper
sauce. *Artichokes with Herb-Butter Sauce:*
globe artichokes act as containers for herb-
butter sauce. *Oriental Deep-Fried Vegetables:*
tempura batter creates a crisp, feather-light
coating for a selection of vegetables, served
with ginger dipping sauce. *Fritto Misto:* deep-fried
vegetables Italian style with breadcrumb-coated
mushrooms and mozzarella sticks accompanying other
batter-fried ingredients. *Swiss Chard Crêpes with Three
Cheeses:* sautéed Swiss chard combines with cheese to fill
crêpes, topped with white cream sauce. *Crêpes with Wild
Mushrooms and Herbs:* crêpes are rolled around a succulent
filling of wild and cultivated
mushrooms. *Cheese-Stuffed
Green Peppers:* in this
version of Mexican
"chiles rellenos"
green peppers
are stuffed
with cheese
and onions
and served
with tomato
salsa. *Red
Peppers Stuffed
with Sweetcorn:*
yellow sweetcorn
and red peppers make
a colourful presentation.
Stir-Fried Thai Vegetables: Thai
seasonings – lemon grass, fish sauce (nam pla), and oyster
sauce – flavour crisp, stir-fried vegetables. *Chinese Stir-Fried
Vegetables:* a different assortment of oriental vegetables is
stir-fried in a Chinese-style sauce. *Aubergine Cannelloni:*
lightly cooked slices of aubergine are rolled around a cheese
filling and fresh basil and baked in thick tomato sauce.
Aubergine Feuilles: an imaginative variation of puff pastry
"milles feuilles" is made with sliced aubergine layered with
cheeses and basil. *Summer Frittata with Ratatouille:*
Italian version of an omelette, cooked with a
ratatouille of late summer vegetables. *Sweetcorn,
Spring Onion, and Red Pepper Frittata:* Yellow
sweetcorn, green spring onions, and red peppers
make an eye-catching combination.

EQUIPMENT

Given the wide range of vegetables and the different methods of preparing them, a variety of equipment is needed. Happily, only a few items are specialized, and in almost all cases just standard kitchen tools are required, such as a colander for draining.

A chef's knife is essential for slicing or chopping large vegetables, with a small knife used for small-to-medium vegetables. The acid in some vegetables will discolour a carbon steel blade, so you may prefer to use a stainless steel serrated knife or a regular blade with a high stainless content. All knives should be sharpened regularly and stored carefully to prevent dulling. The peeler you choose, whether with a fixed or swivel blade, is up to you. You can use a melon baller for hollowing vegetables for stuffing, although a teaspoon also does the job well.

A rolling pin will be needed for some of the quiches and savoury pies in the book. Flan dishes and tins are needed, too; the tin for phyllo pie must have a removable bottom. (It is not advisable to change the size of the tin called for in a recipe because the pastry quantity given will be wrong.) The Mosaic of Vegetables is baked in a terrine mould, and you will need a deep-fat fryer for the Oriental Deep-Fried Vegetables. A pizza stone and paddle come in handy when making pizza, but baking sheets are an excellent alternative. Use a wok for stir-fried vegetables or substitute a large frying pan. A small frying pan works well if you don't have a crêpe pan.

INGREDIENTS

Vegetables combine with a wide array of other ingredients. Fresh herbs such as thyme, tarragon, basil, sage, coriander, and the ubiquitous parsley are always complementary. Spices and seasonings for vegetables range from nutmeg, hot chillies, cayenne, allspice, cinnamon, ginger, cumin, and ground coriander to the more exotic turmeric, fenugreek, and lemon grass. The juice of a lemon brings out the best flavour in almost all vegetables as well as often preventing discoloration. Certain vegetables enhance the flavour of others: almost all will benefit from the addition of onion or shallot, garlic, or tomato.

Cheese makes a winning combination when added to vegetable dishes, whether as a rich filling or a golden topping. Béchamel sauce provides a smooth coating for many main course dishes. Nuts add crunch to a stir-fry, texture to stuffing, and flavour to sauces. Another popular partner is grains: rice, wild rice, and bulghur all form substantial stuffings for baked or braised vegetables. And don't forget, butter and olive and nut oils enhance flavour when frying or sautéing.

TECHNIQUES

Vegetables are so varied that almost every one calls for a specific technique. Some, such as leeks and wild mushrooms, must be cleaned very thoroughly. Artichoke bottoms and whole globe artichokes need careful trimming for cooking. Another basic preparation technique well worth mastering is chopping vegetables, particularly onions, shallots, and garlic, because this is essential to almost all recipes in the book. You will learn as well how to peel peppers, to dice potatoes and courgettes, to cut turnips in julienne strips, and to roll-cut carrots. Preparing vegetables for stuffing is illustrated for a variety of vegetables, including tomatoes, peppers, cabbage leaves, and artichokes, all using different methods.

Turning to cooking, you will see why some vegetables must be blanched and refreshed with cold water, and why some are sprinkled with salt to draw out excess or bitter juices. Boiling and sautéing vegetables to the correct point is clearly illustrated, as is baking and braising vegetables until they are perfectly tender. Coordinating the cooking times of many different vegetables when making soups and stews is explained, as are grilling and shallow- and deep-frying.

As with other volumes in this series, techniques for preparing ingredients other than vegetables are also illustrated in these vegetable recipes. For example, you will find how to prepare chicken stock, how to make coconut milk, and how to make a bouquet garni.

FLEMISH VEGETABLE TART

🍽 SERVES 8   🥣 WORK TIME 50-55 MINUTES*   🍲 BAKING TIME 40-45 MINUTES

EQUIPMENT

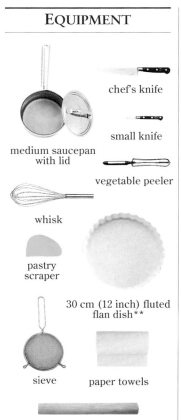

chef's knife

small knife

medium saucepan with lid

vegetable peeler

whisk

pastry scraper

30 cm (12 inch) fluted flan dish**

sieve

paper towels

rolling pin

cling film***

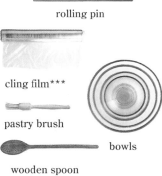

pastry brush

wooden spoon

bowls

chopping board

aluminium foil

**frying pan can also be used
***polythene can also be used

This hearty alternative to pizza uses brioche dough for the crust, with pretty strips of garden vegetables inside. A quick version of brioche is used here, to cut down on work time. For a rustic presentation, bake the tart in a frying pan.

GETTING AHEAD
The brioche dough can be made and refrigerated overnight, but the tart is best eaten the day of baking.

* plus about 1½ hours rising time

metric	SHOPPING LIST	imperial
	For the brioche dough	
9 g	fresh yeast, or 7.5 ml (1½ tsp) dried yeast	⅓ oz
30 ml	lukewarm water	2 tbsp
	vegetable oil for bowl	
250 g	strong plain flour, more if needed	8 oz
5 ml	salt	1 tsp
3	eggs	3
125 g	unsalted butter, softened, more for dish and foil	4 oz
	For the vegetable filling	
500 g	mushrooms	1 lb
8-10	spring onions	8-10
4	medium carrots	4
2	medium turnips	2
90 g	unsalted butter	3 oz
	salt and pepper	
	For the custard	
4	eggs	4
250 ml	double cream	8 fl oz
1.25 ml	ground nutmeg	¼ tsp

INGREDIENTS

fresh yeast

unsalted butter

strong plain flour

mushrooms

eggs

turnips

carrots

spring onions

ground nutmeg

double cream

ORDER OF WORK

1 MAKE THE BRIOCHE DOUGH

2 PREPARE THE VEGETABLES

3 LINE THE FLAN DISH

4 FILL AND BAKE THE TART

1 MAKE THE BRIOCHE DOUGH

1 Crumble or sprinkle the yeast over the water in a small bowl and let stand, 5 minutes. Lightly oil a medium bowl.

2 Sift the flour onto a work surface with the salt. Make a well in the centre and add the yeast mixture and eggs to the well.

Be sure sides of flour well are high enough to contain liquids

Add whole eggs all at once

3 With your fingertips, work the ingredients in the well until thoroughly mixed. Draw in the flour with the pastry scraper and work into the other ingredients with your fingertips to form a smooth dough; add more flour if it is very sticky.

4 Knead the dough on a floured work surface, lifting it up and throwing it down until it is very elastic and resembles chamois leather, about 10 minutes. Work in more flour as necessary, so that at the end of kneading the dough is slightly sticky but peels easily from the work surface.

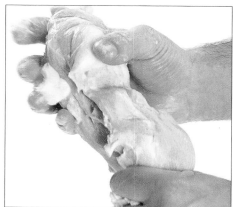

5 Add the butter, and pinch and squeeze to mix it into the dough, then knead on the work surface until smooth again, 3-5 minutes.

ANNE SAYS
"Alternatively, the dough can be kneaded and the butter added using an electric mixer fitted with a dough hook."

6 Shape the dough into a ball and put it into the oiled bowl. Cover it with cling film or oiled polythene and refrigerate about 1 hour. Or, if more convenient, the dough can be left to rise (prove) overnight in the refrigerator.

2 PREPARE THE VEGETABLES

1 Wipe the mushrooms clean with a damp paper towel and trim the stalks level with the caps.

2 Set each mushroom stalk-side down on the chopping board and, with the chef's knife, cut each one into thin vertical slices. Stack the mushroom slices, then cut them across into very thin strips.

3 Trim the root ends from the spring onions and slice them into small pieces.

Guide knife with curled fingers

Hold spring onions together for slicing

4 Peel and trim the carrots and turnips, then cut them into julienne strips (see box, page 13).

5 Melt the butter in the saucepan. Add the carrot julienne strips and cook gently, stirring occasionally, about 5 minutes.

6 Add the mushroom strips and turnip julienne to the saucepan and season with salt and pepper.

How to Cut Vegetables in Julienne Strips

Vegetables cut in julienne strips the size of fine matchsticks are quick to prepare and cook. The principle is much the same for celery, carrots, turnips, courgettes – whatever your selection.

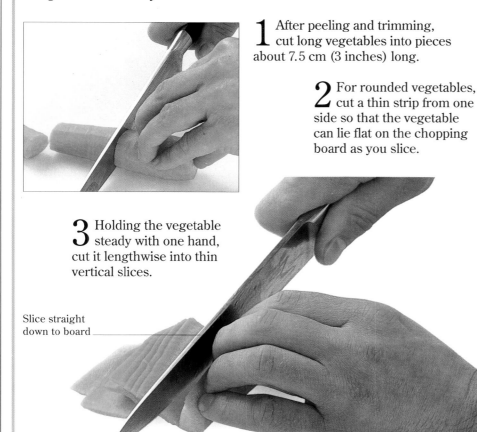

1 After peeling and trimming, cut long vegetables into pieces about 7.5 cm (3 inches) long.

2 For rounded vegetables, cut a thin strip from one side so that the vegetable can lie flat on the chopping board as you slice.

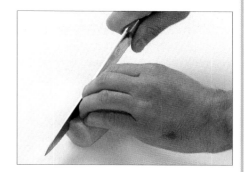

3 Holding the vegetable steady with one hand, cut it lengthwise into thin vertical slices.

Slice straight down to board

4 Stack the slices and cut into fine strips, keeping the tip of the knife on the board as you slice and guiding it with your curled fingers. Use a strip as a guide for length when cutting other vegetables.

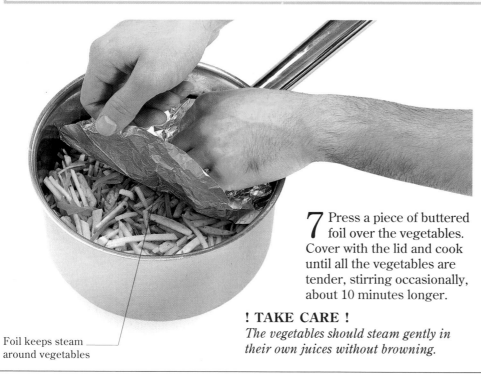

7 Press a piece of buttered foil over the vegetables. Cover with the lid and cook until all the vegetables are tender, stirring occasionally, about 10 minutes longer.

! TAKE CARE !
The vegetables should steam gently in their own juices without browning.

Foil keeps steam around vegetables

8 Remove the saucepan from the heat, add the spring onions, and stir to mix. Taste for seasoning.

3 LINE THE FLAN DISH

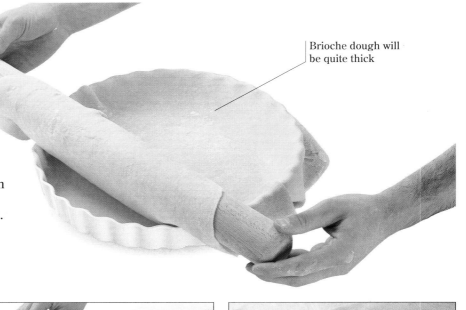

Brioche dough will be quite thick

1 Butter the flan dish. Knead the brioche dough lightly to knock out the air. Lightly flour the work surface, then roll out the brioche dough to a round 7.5 cm (3 inches) larger than the dish. Roll the dough around the rolling pin and drape it over the dish.

! TAKE CARE !
Be careful not to stretch the dough.

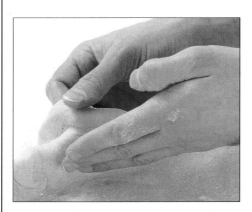

2 Gently lift the edges of the dough with one hand and press it well into the bottom and edge of the flan dish with the other hand.

3 Roll the rolling pin over the top of the dish, pressing down on the pin to cut off the excess dough.

4 With your forefinger and thumb, press the dough evenly up the side, from the bottom, to increase the height of the dough rim.

4 FILL AND BAKE THE TART

Vegetables and custard will not fill dough case completely

Pour custard to cover vegetables evenly

2 Whisk together the eggs, double cream, salt, pepper, and nutmeg. Pour the custard mixture over the vegetables.

ANNE SAYS
"Season the custard mixture well."

1 Heat the oven to 200°C (400°F, Gas 6). Spread the vegetable mixture evenly in the dough case.

Press dough rim gently onto custard filling

3 Fold the top edge of the dough rim over the filling to form a border. Let rise (prove) in a warm place until the dough is puffed, 20-30 minutes.

4 Bake in the heated oven until the brioche case is very brown and the custard is set when tested with the small knife, 40-45 minutes. If the top gets too brown, cover it with foil.

🍽 **TO SERVE**
Serve the tart hot or at room temperature.

Vegetable filling is rich and creamy

Golden crust is quick brioche dough

PISSALADIERE

1 Make the dough as directed.
2 Soak 75 g (2 ½ oz) canned anchovy fillets in 125 ml (4 fl oz) milk, about 1 hour. Drain and halve the fillets lengthwise. Stone 125 g (4 oz) olives.
3 Peel 12 medium onions (total weight about 1.4 kg/3 lb), leaving a little of the root attached, then slice thinly.
4 Strip the leaves from a few sprigs each of fresh thyme and rosemary, pile them on the chopping board, and chop.
5 Heat 60 ml (4 tbsp) olive oil in a frying pan, add the onions, salt, and pepper. Cook until soft, 25-30 minutes, stirring occasionally. Stir in the herbs.
6 Halve 150 g (5 oz) cherry tomatoes.
7 Line the flan dish with the brioche dough as directed, rolling the dough only 2.5 cm (1 inch) larger than the dish. Spread the onions on the bottom.

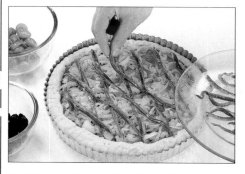

8 Make a diagonal lattice of anchovy fillets on top of the onions. Arrange the cherry tomato halves, cut-side up, and the olives, decoratively on top. Let the tart rise (prove) as directed and bake until brown, 40-45 minutes.
9 Brush the tart with a little olive oil before serving.

THREE-PEPPER PIZZA WITH CHEESE

🍽 SERVES 4-6   🥄 WORK TIME 45-50 MINUTES*   ☕ BAKING TIME 20-25 MINUTES

EQUIPMENT

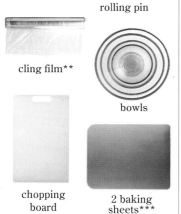

sieve

pastry scraper   frying pan

large metal spoon   small knife

chef's knife

pastry brush

slotted spoon

rolling pin

cling film**

bowls

chopping board   2 baking sheets***

** polythene can also be used
*** pizza paddle and pizza stone can also be used

Ever-popular pizza comes in many shapes and sizes. Here, three colours of peppers topped with mozzarella cheese form a striking display. The pizza dough is made with ground black pepper for a spicy flavour. The peppers should be brightly coloured and firm, with no soft spots.

* plus 1 hour standing time

metric	SHOPPING LIST	imperial
	For the pizza dough	
7.5 ml	dried yeast or 9 g (⅓ oz) fresh yeast	1½ tsp
250 ml	lukewarm water	8 fl oz
375 g	strong plain flour, more if needed	12 oz
2.5 ml	ground black pepper	½ tsp
	salt	
30 ml	olive oil, more for bowl	2 tbsp
	For the topping	
2	medium red peppers	2
1	medium green pepper	1
1	medium yellow pepper	1
2	onions	2
1	small bunch of any fresh herb such as rosemary, thyme, basil, or parsley, or a mixture	1
3	garlic cloves	3
60 ml	olive oil	4 tbsp
	cayenne	
175 g	mozzarella cheese	6 oz

INGREDIENTS

red, green, and yellow peppers

mozzarella cheese   cayenne

strong plain flour

garlic cloves   dried yeast

onions

fresh herbs   olive oil

ANNE SAYS
"When shopping for fresh herbs, look for healthy sprigs that have a strong fragrance. Avoid bouquets with dried ends, discoloured leaves, or wilted stalks."

ORDER OF WORK

1 MAKE THE PIZZA DOUGH

2 PREPARE THE TOPPING

3 ASSEMBLE AND BAKE THE PIZZA

1 MAKE THE PIZZA DOUGH

Pastry scraper draws flour in easily

1 Sprinkle or crumble the yeast over 30-45 ml (2-3 tbsp) of the water and let stand until dissolved, about 5 minutes. Lightly oil a large bowl.

2 Sift the flour onto a work surface with the black pepper and 1.25 ml (1/4 tsp) salt. Make a well in the centre and add the yeast mixture with the remaining water and the olive oil. Work the ingredients in the well with your fingertips, until thoroughly mixed.

3 Draw in the flour with the pastry scraper and work into the other ingredients with your fingertips to form a smooth dough; add more flour if the dough is very sticky.

HOW TO CORE AND DESEED PEPPERS AND CUT THEM INTO STRIPS OR DICE

The cores and seeds of peppers must always be discarded before use.

1 With a small knife, cut around each pepper core. Twist the cores and then carefully pull them out. Halve the peppers lengthwise and scrape out the seeds. Cut away the white ribs on the inside of the peppers.

Cut round core neatly so it can be pulled away easily

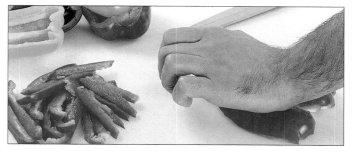

2 Set each pepper half cut-side down on the work surface and press down on the top of the pepper half with the heel of your hand, to flatten it for easier slicing.

3 With a chef's knife, slice each pepper half lengthwise into strips. For dice, gather the strips together in a pile and cut across.

4 Holding one end of the dough with one hand, press firmly down into the dough with the heel of your other hand, pushing away from you. Peel it back from the work surface in one piece, shape into a loose ball, and turn 90 degrees. Continue kneading until it is smooth and elastic, 5-8 minutes.

ANNE SAYS
"A good alternative to mixing and kneading the pizza dough by hand is to use an electric mixer which has been fitted with a dough hook."

Kneading develops gluten in dough, so it is elastic and even-textured

5 Transfer the dough to the oiled bowl, cover it with cling film or oiled polythene, and let rise (prove) in a warm place until doubled in bulk, about 1 hour.

ANNE SAYS
"Alternatively, the dough can be left to rise overnight in the refrigerator."

2 PREPARE THE TOPPING

1 Core and deseed the red, green, and yellow peppers and cut them into strips (see box, page 17).

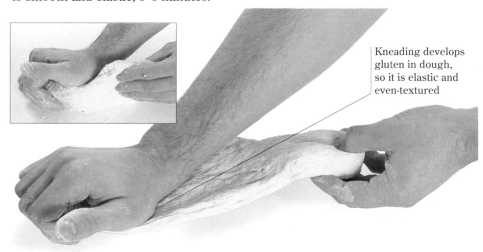

Brightly coloured peppers should be sliced thinly for quick cooking

Use bent fingers to guide knife

2 Peel the onions, leaving a little of the root attached, and cut them in half through root and stalk. Lay each onion half flat on the chopping board and cut vertically into thin slices.

ANNE SAYS
"The root holds the onion together."

3 Strip the herb leaves from the sprigs, pile on the chopping board, and finely chop. Finely chop the garlic (see box, page 20).

4 Heat 15 ml (1 tbsp) of the oil in the frying pan, add the onions, and cook, stirring, until soft but not brown, 2-3 minutes. Transfer to a bowl and set aside.

5 Add the remaining oil to the pan, then the peppers, garlic, and half of the herbs. Season with salt and cayenne. Sauté, stirring, until the peppers are softened but not brown, 7-10 minutes. Taste for seasoning: the mixture should be quite spicy. Let cool. Slice the mozzarella.

3 ASSEMBLE AND BAKE THE PIZZA

1 Heat the oven to 230°C (450°F, Gas 8). Put one baking sheet near the bottom of the oven to heat.

Dough will shrink as it is rolled, so treat it firmly

2 Knead the dough lightly to knock out the air, then shape into a ball. Lightly flour the work surface. Roll the dough into a round. Pull and slap it until the round is 1 cm (¹/₂ inch) thick.

3 Generously flour the second baking sheet. Transfer the dough round to the sheet and press up the edge to form a shallow rim.

4 Spread the onions and then the peppers on the pizza base, leaving a 2 cm (³/₄ inch) border. Spoon any remaining oil from the pan over the peppers and top with the mozzarella. Let stand in a warm place until the dough is puffed, 10-15 minutes.

Dough rim keeps in juices from topping

HOW TO PEEL AND CHOP GARLIC

The strength of garlic varies with its age and dryness; use more when it is very fresh.

1 To separate garlic cloves, crush a bulb with the heel of your hand. Or, pull a clove from the bulb with your fingers. To peel the clove, lightly crush it with the flat side of a chef's knife to loosen the skin.

2 Peel off the skin from the garlic clove with your fingers.

3 To crush the clove, set the flat side of a knife on top and strike firmly with your fist. Finely chop the garlic with the knife, moving the blade back and forth.

5 With a sharp jerking movement, slide the pizza onto the heated baking sheet. Bake in the heated oven until browned, 20-25 minutes.

ANNE SAYS
"Putting the pizza onto a hot baking sheet ensures that the pizza base will cook thoroughly."

Slip away sheet with sharp jerk

🍴 TO SERVE
Sprinkle the pizza with the reserved herbs and cut it into slices.

Pepper topping is sweet and spicy

Mozzarella cheese adds richness to pizza

GETTING AHEAD
The pizza dough can be made and the peppers can be prepared up to 12 hours ahead and kept refrigerated. Assemble the pizza and bake it just before serving.

MUSHROOM
AND ARTICHOKE PIZZAS

*Sautéed mushrooms and artichokes,
moistened with tomato sauce,
form the topping for these
20 cocktail-size pizzas.*

1 Make the pizza dough as directed, omitting the pepper.
2 Prepare 4 medium globe artichoke bottoms. Half-fill a pan with water, add salt, then the artichokes. Weigh them down with a heatproof plate, bring to a boil, and simmer until tender, 15-20 minutes. Drain the artichokes and let cool to tepid. Scoop out the chokes with a teaspoon and cut bottoms into wedges. Alternatively, you can use canned artichoke bottoms, well drained, to save time.
3 Peel, deseed, and chop 750 g (1½ lb) tomatoes. Peel and finely chop 1 large onion and 3 garlic cloves. Heat 45 ml (3 tbsp) olive oil in a frying pan, add the onion, and cook until soft but not brown, 3-4 minutes. Add the tomatoes, garlic, 45 ml (3 tbsp) tomato purée, 1 bouquet garni, a small pinch of sugar, salt, and pepper. Cover and cook over low heat 10 minutes. Uncover and cook, stirring occasionally, until sauce is thick, about 15 minutes. Taste for seasoning.
4 Grate 125 g (4 oz) Gruyère cheese.
5 Wipe 125 g (4 oz) mushrooms with a damp paper towel and trim the stalks even with the caps. Set the mushrooms stalk-side down and slice them.
6 Sauté the mushrooms and artichokes as for the peppers, with the garlic and herbs, using 30 ml (2 tbsp) olive oil.
7 Roll and pull out the dough to 5 mm (¼ inch) thick and cut it into shapes using a 10 cm (4 inch) pastry cutter (a flower-shaped cutter was used for the photograph).
8 Spread an even layer of tomato sauce over each pizza base, arrange the artichoke hearts and mushrooms on top, and sprinkle with the grated Gruyère. Let rise (prove) and then bake 10-15 minutes.
9 Arrange on a serving plate; decorate with parsley sprigs.

THREE-PEPPER CALZONE
WITH CHEESE

*The pizza dough and filling
are reassembled in the shape of
a turnover in this recipe,
which serves 4.*

1 Make the pizza dough as directed.
2 Prepare the topping as directed, and mix the onions and pepper strips together.
3 Divide the dough into 4 equal pieces. Roll and pull each piece into a square about 1 cm (½ inch) thick.

4 Spoon the pepper mixture onto a diagonal half of each square, leaving a 2.5 cm (1 inch) border. Arrange the mozzarella slices on top of the pepper mixture.
5 Moisten the edge of each square with water and fold one corner over to meet the other, forming a triangle.
6 Pinch the edges together to seal them. Put the triangles on the floured baking sheet and let rise (prove). Whisk 1 egg with 2.5 ml (½ tsp) salt and brush this glaze over the calzone, marking a lattice on the floured surface. Bake them until golden brown, 15-20 minutes.
7 Brush each with a little olive oil and serve.

BROCCOLI AND MUSHROOM QUICHE

🍴 SERVES 6-8   🥄 WORK TIME 45-50 MINUTES*   🍲 BAKING TIME 30-35 MINUTES

EQUIPMENT

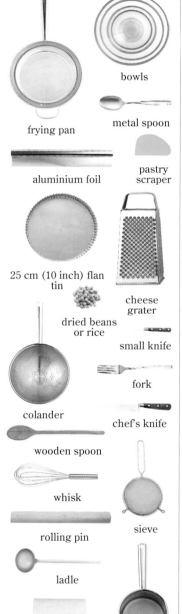

bowls

frying pan

metal spoon

aluminium foil

pastry scraper

25 cm (10 inch) flan tin

cheese grater

dried beans or rice

small knife

fork

colander

chef's knife

wooden spoon

whisk

rolling pin

sieve

ladle

paper towels   large saucepan

metal skewer

Quiche, the savoury pie from Alsace, has swept the world. This version features pieces of broccoli on a bed of sautéed mushrooms. Look for broccoli with firm stalks that are not dried out.

* plus 45 minutes standing time

metric	SHOPPING LIST	imperial
1-2	heads of broccoli, total weight about 500 g (1 lb)	1-2
	salt and pepper	
175 g	mushrooms	6 oz
2	garlic cloves	2
30 g	butter	1 oz
	ground nutmeg	
	For the pastry dough	
200 g	plain flour	6½ oz
1	egg yolk	1
2.5 ml	salt	½ tsp
45 ml	water, more if needed	3 tbsp
100 g	unsalted butter, more for flan tin	3½ oz
	For the cheese custard	
3	eggs	3
2	egg yolks	2
375 ml	milk	12 fl oz
250 ml	double cream	8 fl oz
60 g	grated Parmesan cheese	2 oz
	ground nutmeg	

INGREDIENTS

mushrooms   broccoli

ground nutmeg   plain flour

garlic cloves

grated Parmesan cheese

milk

eggs

butter

egg yolks   double cream

ORDER OF WORK

1 MAKE THE PASTRY DOUGH

2 LINE THE TIN

3 BAKE THE PASTRY SHELL BLIND

4 COOK THE VEGETABLES

5 ASSEMBLE AND BAKE THE QUICHE

1 MAKE THE PASTRY DOUGH

1 Sift the flour onto a work surface and make a well in the centre. Put the egg yolk, salt, and water in the well.

Your fingertips are ideal for mixing

2 Using the rolling pin, pound the butter to soften it slightly, then add it to the well in the flour. Using your fingertips, work the ingredients in the well until thoroughly mixed.

3 Draw in the flour with the pastry scraper. With your fingers, work the flour into the other ingredients until coarse crumbs form. Press the dough into a ball.

ANNE SAYS
"*If the dough is very dry, sprinkle it with more water.*"

Knead dough until it is very pliable

4 Lightly flour the work surface, then blend the dough by pushing it away from you with the heel of your hand. Gather it up with the pastry scraper and continue to blend until it is very smooth and peels away from the work surface in one piece, 1-2 minutes.

5 Shape the pastry dough into a ball, wrap it tightly, and chill until firm, about 30 minutes.

2 LINE THE TIN

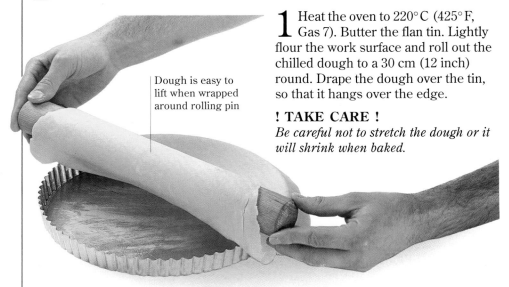

Dough is easy to
lift when wrapped
around rolling pin

1 Heat the oven to 220°C (425°F, Gas 7). Butter the flan tin. Lightly flour the work surface and roll out the chilled dough to a 30 cm (12 inch) round. Drape the dough over the tin, so that it hangs over the edge.

! TAKE CARE !
Be careful not to stretch the dough or it will shrink when baked.

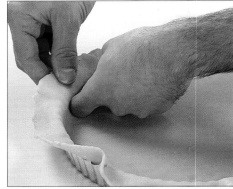

2 Gently lift the edge of the dough with one hand and press it well into the bottom edge of the tin with the forefinger of the other hand.

3 Roll the rolling pin over the top of the tin, pressing down on the pin to cut off the excess dough.

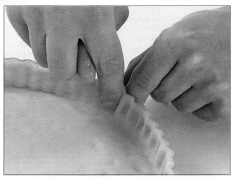

4 With your forefingers and thumb, press the dough evenly up the side, from the bottom, to increase the height of the dough rim.

5 Prick the bottom of the shell with the fork to prevent air bubbles from forming during baking. Chill until firm, at least 15 minutes.

3 BAKE THE PASTRY SHELL BLIND

1 Line the pastry dough shell with a double thickness of foil, pressing it well into the bottom edge. If necessary, trim the foil so it stands about 4 cm (1½ inches) above the edge of the tin.

Foil supports dough
so it does not lose
shape in baking

2 Spread a layer of dried beans or rice on the foil to weigh down the dough while it is baking.

3 Bake the pastry dough shell until set and starting to brown, about 15 minutes. While the pastry shell is baking, cook the vegetables. Remove the foil and beans; reduce the oven heat to 190°C (375°F, Gas 5).

4 Continue baking until the pastry is lightly browned, about 5 minutes longer. Remove the pastry shell from the oven and test with your hand whether the pastry is set. Set aside; leave the oven on.

4 COOK THE VEGETABLES

1 Trim the broccoli, leaving about 5 cm (2 inches) of stalk. With the small knife, strip the tough outer skin from the stalk.

Drain broccoli as soon as it is tender

Use colander to drain broccoli thoroughly

2 Cut the florets from the stalk where they begin to branch. Slice the stalk lengthwise into sticks.

3 Half-fill the saucepan with water and bring to a boil. Add salt, then add the broccoli. Cook until just tender, 3-5 minutes. Drain, rinse with cold water, and drain again thoroughly.

HOW TO CLEAN AND SLICE MUSHROOMS

Mushrooms need to be cleaned carefully if they are dirty. Be sure to rinse them in water only 1-2 seconds; do not soak because they quickly become waterlogged.

1 Wipe the mushrooms clean with a damp paper towel or cloth. If they are very dirty, plunge them into cold water, swirl around, and lift out to drain in a colander.

2 With a small knife, trim the stalks just level with the caps. If using wild mushrooms, trim just the ends of the stalks.

3 To slice, hold the mushrooms stalk-side down and cut them vertically with a chef's knife into slices of the required thickness.

4 Clean and slice the mushrooms (see box, left). Set the flat side of the chef's knife on top of each garlic clove and strike it with your fist. Discard the skin and finely chop the garlic cloves.

5 Melt the butter in the frying pan. Add the mushrooms, garlic, salt, pepper, and a pinch of nutmeg. Cook, stirring, until the liquid has evaporated, about 5 minutes. Taste for seasoning.

! TAKE CARE !
Cook the mushrooms until quite dry or they may curdle the filling.

5 ASSEMBLE AND BAKE THE QUICHE

1 Make the cheese custard: whisk together the eggs, egg yolks, milk, cream, grated cheese, salt, pepper, and a pinch of nutmeg in a small bowl.

2 Using the metal spoon, spread the sautéed mushrooms on the bottom of the pastry shell. Arrange the broccoli florets and sticks of broccoli stalk on top in concentric circles.

Make neat pattern with broccoli in pastry shell

3 Ladle the cheese custard over the vegetables to fill the pastry shell almost to the rim.

Broccoli florets show temptingly through custard

4 Bake the quiche in the oven until browned and the cheese custard is set when tested with the metal skewer, 30-35 minutes.

ANNE SAYS
"The skewer inserted in the centre of the quiche should come out clean."

🍴 TO SERVE
Cut the quiche into wedges and serve hot or at room temperature.

Parmesan-flavoured custard holds tender pieces of broccoli and mushroom

Pastry is crisp and buttery

V A R I A T I O N

COURGETTE AND MUSHROOM QUICHE

Rounds of courgette replace the broccoli in this quiche.

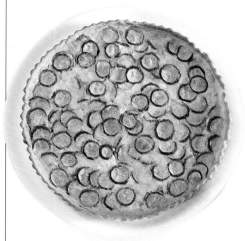

1 Make the pastry dough. Line and bake blind the pastry shell as directed.
2 Trim 3 medium courgettes (total weight about 375 g/12 oz) and cut them into 5 cm (2 inch) slices. Half-fill a saucepan with water. Bring to a boil, add salt, and blanch the courgettes until just tender, 1-2 minutes. Drain, rinse with cold water, then pat the slices dry with paper towels.
3 Cook the mushrooms and prepare the cheese custard as directed.
4 Assemble the quiche, arranging the courgette slices attractively on top of the mushrooms. Pour the custard over the vegetables and bake as directed.

—— GETTING AHEAD ——
The quiche can be made 2 days ahead and kept, tightly covered, in the refrigerator. Reheat it in a 180°C (350°F, Gas 4) oven for 10-15 minutes before serving.

PHYLLO PIE WITH SPICY KALE AND SAUSAGE

 SERVES 6   WORK TIME 35-40 MINUTES   BAKING TIME 45-55 MINUTES

EQUIPMENT

chef's knife

wooden spoon

slotted spoon

fork

pastry brush

colander

kitchen scissors

bowls

sauté pan with lid*

small saucepan

chopping board

28 cm (11 inch) round loose-based flan tin

tea towels

*frying pan with lid can also be used

Based on the Greek spinach pie, "spanokopita", this recipe combines kale with onions, spice, and sausage meat inside a package of golden brown flaky phyllo pastry. Other hearty greens can be substituted for the kale in the filling: spring greens or even spinach can be used instead. Choose young greens with small tender leaves, avoiding tough woody stalks which show old age.

GETTING AHEAD

The pie can be prepared, wrapped securely, and kept in the refrigerator up to 2 days; it also freezes well. Bake just before serving.

metric	SHOPPING LIST	imperial
175 g	butter	6 oz
500 g	package phyllo dough	1 lb
	For the kale and sausage filling	
750 g	kale	1½ lb
3	medium onions	3
250 g	sausage meat	8 oz
30 g	butter	1 oz
2.5 ml	ground allspice	½ tsp
	salt and pepper	
2	eggs	2

INGREDIENTS

kale   eggs

onions   butter

phyllo dough

sausage meat

ground allspice

ANNE SAYS
"For a vegetarian phyllo pie, the sausage meat can be omitted from the filling."

ORDER OF WORK

1 PREPARE THE VEGETABLES FOR THE FILLING

2 COOK THE INGREDIENTS FOR THE FILLING

3 ASSEMBLE AND BAKE THE PIE

1 PREPARE THE VEGETABLES FOR THE FILLING

Loosely rolling kale makes cutting easy

1 Using the colander, wash the kale thoroughly, then discard any thick stalks. Take a few leaves of kale at a time, roll them up loosely, and cut across into thin strips. Chop the onions (see box, below).

HOW TO CHOP AN ONION

An onion can be sliced, then cut into even dice or chopped more finely if this is called for in a recipe. The size of dice depends on the thickness of the initial onion slices. For a standard size, make slices that are about 5 mm (¼ inch) thick. For finely chopped onions, slice as thinly as possible.

1 Peel the onion and trim the top; leave a little of the root attached to hold the onion together.

2 Cut the onion lengthwise in half, through root and stalk.

3 Put one half, cut-side down, on the chopping board and hold the onion steady with one hand. Using a chef's knife, make a series of horizontal cuts from the top towards the root (but not through it).

4 Make a series of lengthwise vertical cuts, cutting just to the root but not through it.

ANNE SAYS
"When slicing, tuck your fingertips under and use your knuckles to guide the blade of the knife."

5 Slice the onion crosswise into dice. For finely chopped onion, continue chopping until you have the fineness required.

Neat dice are easily obtained this way

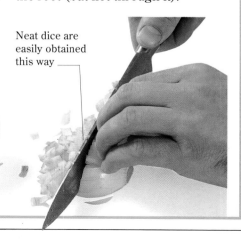

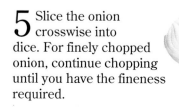

2 COOK THE INGREDIENTS FOR THE FILLING

Lightly fried sausage meat has crumbly texture

1 If necessary, remove the sausage meat from its casing and crumble it. Heat the butter in the sauté pan, add the sausage, and cook, stirring, until it is crumbly and brown, 3-5 minutes.

2 Transfer the sausage meat to a bowl with the slotted spoon, leaving the sausage fat behind.

Stir constantly with wooden spoon

3 Add the onions to the pan and cook, stirring, until soft.

ANNE SAYS
"You may have to add the kale in batches, adding more as each batch softens."

Kale retains vivid green colour

4 Add the kale strips, then cover with the lid and cook very gently until the kale is wilted, 3-5 minutes. Remove the lid and cook, stirring constantly, until the moisture has evaporated, about 5 minutes.

Sausage meat adds richness to filling

5 Return the sausage meat to the pan with the allspice and stir into the kale mixture. Season to taste with salt and plenty of pepper. Remove from the heat and let cool completely.

6 Lightly beat the eggs with the fork and stir them into the filling.

3 ASSEMBLE AND BAKE THE PIE

Work quickly with phyllo dough so it does not dry out

1 Heat the oven to 180°C (350°F, Gas 4). Melt the butter in the saucepan; brush the flan tin with a little of the butter.

2 Lay a folded damp tea towel on the work surface. Unroll the phyllo dough sheets onto the towel.

3 Using the flan tin as a guide, cut through the pastry sheets to leave a 7.5 cm (3 inch) border around the tin where possible. Reserve the trimmings for garnish. Cover the sheets and trimmings with a second folded damp towel.

! TAKE CARE !
Do not let the phyllo dough dry out or it will be hard to work with.

Handle dough gently
to avoid tearing it

4 Put 1 phyllo sheet on top of a
third damp towel and brush the
phyllo lightly with butter. Transfer
the buttered sheet to the flan tin,
pressing it well into the side.

A few creases in
dough do not matter

5 Butter another
phyllo sheet and
put it in the tin at a
right angle to the first.
Continue buttering and
layering until half of the
phyllo is used, arranging each
alternate layer at right angles.

Spoon in filling,
still working
quickly

6 Spoon the kale and
sausage meat filling
into the phyllo dough case
and spread it out evenly over
the bottom of the case
with the back of the spoon.

7 Butter another sheet of phyllo
dough and cover the filling with
it. Top with the remaining sheets of
phyllo, brushing each, including the
top one, with melted butter.

8 Fold the overhanging dough up around the edge of the pie top, tucking it around your finger and pressing it around the edge of the tin, pinching with fingers and thumbs to form ridges.

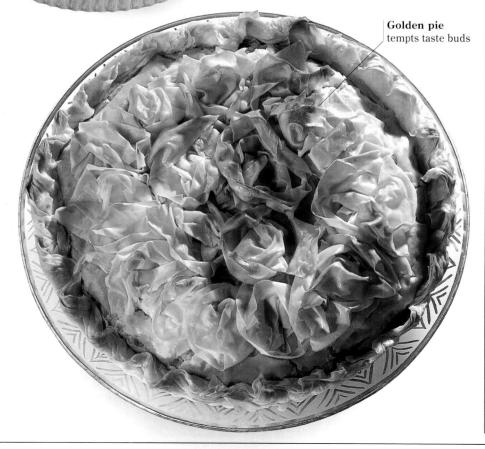

Deft touch will ensure dough adheres easily

9 Cut the phyllo dough trimmings into 5 cm (2 inch) wide strips. Pleat them to form ruffles and arrange on top of the pie so it is completely covered. Drizzle the remaining melted butter over the top. Bake the pie in the heated oven until golden brown, 45-55 minutes. Let the pie cool slightly, then cut into wedges and serve hot or at room temperature.

! TAKE CARE !
If the pie browns too quickly, cover it with a piece of foil.

Golden pie tempts taste buds

VARIATION

POTATO AND BLUE CHEESE PHYLLO PIE

1 Peel 1 kg (2 lb) potatoes and cut them into very thin slices. Cover them with a damp towel.

2 Separate 4 shallots into sections, and peel. Using a small knife, slice each section horizontally towards the root, leaving the slices attached at the root. Slice vertically, still leaving the root end uncut, then across to make fine dice.

3 Strip the leaves from a few sprigs each of fresh parsley, tarragon, and chervil and pile them on the chopping board. With the chef's knife, finely chop the leaves.

4 Trim the rind from 125 g (4 oz) blue cheese, then crumble it. Cut 125 g (4 oz) bacon into strips. Heat 15 ml (1 tbsp) butter in a frying pan, add the bacon, and cook until brown, about 5 minutes. Drain on paper towels.

5 Trim the phyllo sheets and line the flan tin with half of the sheets as directed. Arrange half of the potatoes in an overlapping layer in the flan tin. Sprinkle with half of the blue cheese, bacon strips, chopped shallots, herbs, salt, and pepper. Repeat with the remaining potatoes, cheese, bacon, shallots, and herbs.

6 Cover the pie with the remaining phyllo sheets, buttering each one. Cut a 7.5 cm (3 inch) circle from the centre of the dough lid using a pastry cutter or glass, so the filling shows through.

7 Finish the pie with the dough strips and bake as directed. While still hot, spoon 45-60 ml (3-4 tbsp) soured cream into the centre of the pie and serve.

4 Cut the cores from the tomatoes and score an "x" on the base of each with the tip of a knife. Immerse them in a pan of boiling water until the skin starts to split, 8-15 seconds depending on ripeness. Transfer them at once to a bowl of cold water. When cold, peel off the skin.

5 With the chef's knife, cut the tomatoes crosswise in half and squeeze out the seeds, then coarsely chop each half. Drain the canned chick peas in the sieve and rinse them thoroughly with cold water.

6 Heat the oil in a large saucepan, add the onion, and cook, stirring with the wooden spoon, until soft but not brown, 2-3 minutes. Add the tomatoes and cook, stirring, until thickened, about 5 minutes.

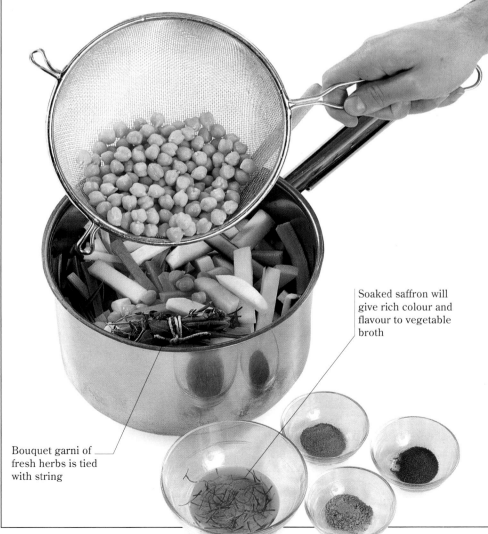

7 Add the chicken stock to the onion and tomatoes with the courgettes, carrot, and turnip sticks, the leeks, bouquet garni, and chick peas. Stir in the ginger, turmeric, paprika, saffron with its liquid, salt, and pepper.

Soaked saffron will give rich colour and flavour to vegetable broth

Bouquet garni of fresh herbs is tied with string

8 Bring to a boil and simmer until the vegetables are just tender, 15-20 minutes. Discard the bouquet garni. Taste the broth for seasoning.

2 PREPARE THE VEGETABLE KEBABS

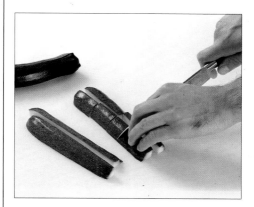  

1 Trim the courgettes. Cut each one lengthwise into quarters, then across into 4 cm (1½ inch) pieces.

2 With a sharp movement, twist the cores out of the red peppers, then halve the peppers and scrape out the seeds. Cut peppers into large squares.

3 Wipe the mushroom caps with a damp paper towel and trim the stalks level with the caps. Cut the mushrooms vertically in half, or into quarters if large.

4 Cut the onions into quarters, leaving on a little root to hold them together. Pick over the cherry tomatoes. Or, cut medium tomatoes into quarters, then cut the quarters crosswise in half.

Choose small onions to make vegetable skewers attractive

Herb and oil marinade gives delicious flavour to vegetables

5 Strip the coriander and thyme leaves from the stalks and pile them on the chopping board. With the chef's knife, finely chop the leaves. Set aside 15-30 ml (1-2 tbsp) for sprinkling before serving; put the remainder in a small bowl and mix in the olive oil.

6 Put the mushrooms, courgettes, red peppers, onions, and tomatoes in a large bowl. Pour the herb and olive oil mixture over the vegetables.

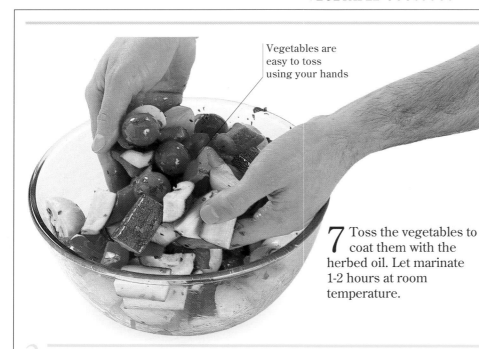

Vegetables are easy to toss using your hands

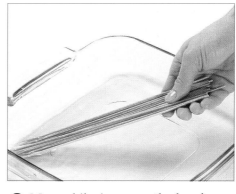

7 Toss the vegetables to coat them with the herbed oil. Let marinate 1-2 hours at room temperature.

8 Meanwhile, immerse the bamboo skewers in water in the shallow dish and set aside to soak.

ANNE SAYS
"*Soaking prevents bamboo skewers from burning when grilled.*"

3 GRILL THE KEBABS AND PREPARE THE COUSCOUS

2 Set the kebabs on the oiled baking sheet and grill them about 7.5 cm (3 inches) from the heat until browned, about 5 minutes. Turn the kebabs and grill on the other side until browned and tender, about 5 minutes longer.

Leave ends of skewers free so you can pick them up

1 Heat the grill. Take the soaked skewers from the water and thread the vegetables onto them, alternating the red pepper, mushroom, courgettes, tomatoes, and onion. Scrape any herbs from the bowl; brush on the kebabs.

Alternate vegetables to give contrast in colour

3 While the kebabs are grilling, prepare the couscous: put the couscous in a large bowl and pour the boiling water over it, stirring quickly with the fork. Let the couscous sit until plump, about 5 minutes.

ANNE SAYS
"*The quantity of boiling water required may vary with the couscous you use, so check the package directions.*"

VARIATION
FISH COUSCOUS

VARIATION
VEGETABLE AND LAMB COUSCOUS

4 Add the butter, salt, and pepper to the couscous. Stir and toss with the fork to fluff the grains and incorporate the butter. Taste for seasoning.

🍴 TO SERVE

Reheat the vegetable broth if necessary and transfer it to a deep serving bowl. Pile the couscous on a warmed serving plate. Sprinkle the kebabs with salt, pepper, cumin, and the reserved chopped herbs. Arrange the skewers in the centre of the couscous; serve with fiery harissa (Moroccan hot sauce).

1 Cut 1 kg (2 lb) monkfish fillets into even-sized 5 cm (2 inch) pieces.
2 Make the vegetable broth as directed, using water in place of the chicken stock and replacing the ground ginger with 7.5 ml (1½ tsp) ground cumin. After simmering 5-10 minutes, add the monkfish pieces and continue simmering gently until the fish is flaky and the vegetables are tender, 10-12 minutes longer.
3 Omit the vegetable kebabs, and prepare the couscous as directed.
4 Divide the couscous among warmed individual dishes. Put the hot broth into a well made in the centre of each serving and arrange the fish around the edge. Decorate with parsley.

1 Bring a large pan of water to a boil and add 1 kg (2 lb) lamb or veal bones, cut into pieces. Return to a boil; simmer 5 minutes. Drain and rinse the bones.
2 Make the vegetable broth as directed, using water instead of chicken stock and adding the blanched bones with the water. Do not yet add the vegetable sticks, chick peas, or spices. Simmer, skimming occasionally, 45-60 minutes.
3 Trim the fat from 500 g (1 lb) boneless lamb shoulder; cut meat into 2.5 cm (1 inch) cubes.
4 Prepare the mushrooms, red peppers, and onions for the kebabs, omitting the courgettes and tomatoes. Add the lamb cubes with the herbs and oil. Toss and let marinate 1-2 hours.
5 Strain the broth. Add the vegetable sticks with the chick peas and spices and continue cooking as directed.
6 Thread the red peppers, lamb cubes, onion, and mushroom onto the skewers and grill, 4-5 minutes per side. Sprinkle with the cumin, chopped chives, salt, and pepper.
7 Prepare the couscous as directed. Divide it among warmed individual shallow dishes. Put the hot vegetable broth into a well made in the centre of each serving and the kebabs on top. Decorate with parsley.

Vegetable broth is warmly spiced

Vegetable kebabs are flavoured with fresh herbs

GETTING AHEAD

The broth can be made up to 2 days in advance and kept, covered, in the refrigerator, or it can be frozen. The kebabs and couscous are best cooked just before serving.

GENOESE MINESTRONE

🍽️ SERVES 6 🥄 WORK TIME 1½ -2 HOURS 🍲 COOKING TIME ¾-1 HOUR

EQUIPMENT

A purée of tomato, garlic, and basil is stirred in at the finish to give a burst of fresh flavour to Genoese-style minestrone.

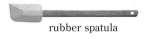

food processor**

colander

slotted spoon

cheese grater

bowls

saucepans

wooden spoon

small knife

ladle

vegetable peeler   chef's knife

rubber spatula

chopping board

** blender can also be used

GETTING AHEAD
The soup and sauce can be made 1 day ahead and refrigerated separately; reheat soup before adding sauce.

* plus 8 hours soaking time

metric	SHOPPING LIST	imperial
175 g	dried red kidney beans	6 oz
175 g	dried cannellini beans	6 oz
125 g	elbow macaroni	4 oz
175 g	French beans	6 oz
3	carrots, total weight about 250 g (8 oz)	3
3	potatoes, total weight about 375 g (12 oz)	3
1	medium courgette	1
175 g	shelled fresh peas or defrosted peas	6 oz
	salt and pepper	
2 litres	water	3¼ pints
125 g	grated Parmesan cheese for sprinkling	4 oz
For the tomato pesto sauce		
2	medium tomatoes	2
1	large bunch of fresh basil	1
4	garlic cloves	4
5 ml	salt	1 tsp
	pepper	
175 ml	olive oil	6 fl oz

INGREDIENTS

courgette

dried red kidney beans

French beans

dried cannellini beans

garlic cloves

fresh basil

peas

elbow macaroni

potatoes

Parmesan cheese

tomatoes

olive oil   carrots

ORDER OF WORK

1 PREPARE THE DRIED BEANS AND MACARONI

2 MAKE THE VEGETABLE SOUP

3 MAKE THE TOMATO PESTO SAUCE

4 FINISH THE SOUP

1 PREPARE THE DRIED BEANS AND MACARONI

1 Put the kidney and cannellini beans in separate bowls. Add water to cover generously and leave them to soak overnight. Drain the beans, rinse with cold water, and drain again.

ANNE SAYS
"Rather than soaking the beans overnight, you can put them in 2 medium saucepans with water to cover, bring to a boil, and let simmer 1 hour, adding more water if necessary so the beans are always covered."

2 Put the beans in separate saucepans, add water to cover generously, and bring to a boil. Reduce the heat and simmer. Season with salt and pepper halfway through cooking. Cook the beans until tender but still slightly firm when gently squeezed, about 1½ hours. Drain thoroughly.

! TAKE CARE !
Salt added at the beginning of cooking toughens the skin of dried beans.

Water washes away starch so pasta does not stick together

3 Fill a medium saucepan with water, bring to a boil, and add salt. Add the macaroni and cook until just tender, stirring occasionally, 5-7 minutes. Drain and rinse with hot water, then set aside.

2 MAKE THE VEGETABLE SOUP

1 Break the ends off the French beans and cut the beans into 1 cm (½ inch) pieces. Peel the carrots and potatoes; trim the ends from the courgette. Cut the carrots, potatoes, and courgette into dice (see box, right).

Chef's knife helps you dice quickly

HOW TO DICE VEGETABLES

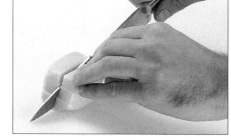

1 Peel or trim the vegetable, then square off the sides. Cut vertically into 1 cm (½ inch) slices.

2 Stack the slices together and cut downwards through the slices to make 1 cm (½ inch) strips.

3 Gather the strips together into a pile and cut them crosswise to produce even 1 cm (½ inch) dice.

Keep fingers out of blade's way

Add peas to colourful mixture of vegetables in pan

2 Put the cooked beans in a large saucepan and add the French beans, carrots, potatoes, courgette, peas, and a little salt and pepper.

3 Add the water and bring to a boil, then reduce the heat and simmer over low heat until the vegetables are very tender, 1 hour. Meanwhile, make the tomato pesto sauce.

3 MAKE THE TOMATO PESTO SAUCE

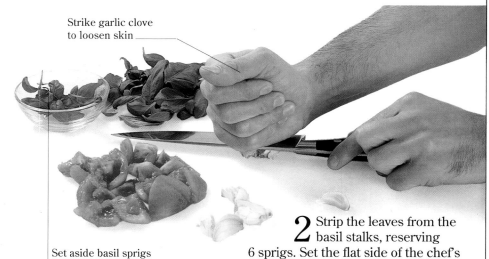

Strike garlic clove to loosen skin

Set aside basil sprigs for herb garnish

1 Score an "x" on the base of each tomato. Immerse them in boiling water until skin starts to split. Transfer to cold water, then peel. Halve the tomatoes, squeeze out seeds, and chop.

2 Strip the leaves from the basil stalks, reserving 6 sprigs. Set the flat side of the chef's knife on top of each garlic clove and strike it with your fist. Discard skin.

3 Put the garlic, basil leaves, and chopped tomatoes, salt, and a little pepper in the food processor and purée until the mixture is smooth.

Tomatoes add flavour and help stabilize the sauce

4 With the blades turning, gradually add the oil. Scrape down the sides of the processor bowl from time to time with the rubber spatula. Taste the sauce for seasoning.

4 FINISH THE SOUP

Pesto sauce flavours soup and thickens it slightly

1 Add the macaroni to the vegetable soup and taste for seasoning. Gently reheat the soup to boiling. Remove the saucepan from the heat, and stir the tomato pesto sauce into the minestrone soup.

Freshly grated Parmesan cheese enhances flavour of vegetables

🍴 TO SERVE

Ladle the soup into warmed soup bowls, top each serving with a basil sprig, and serve the freshly grated Parmesan cheese separately.

Vegetables in minestrone are meltingly tender

V A R I A T I O N

SOUPE AU PISTOU, CROUTES GRATINEES

With a few changes, Genoese Minestrone becomes the famous French soup, Pistou.

1 Cook the dried beans and macaroni, and make the vegetable soup as directed, omitting the peas.
2 Make the tomato pesto sauce as directed.
3 Heat the oven to 180°C (350°F, Gas 4). Make toasted cheese croûtes: cut 1 small loaf of French bread (weighing about 175 g/6 oz) into 24 slices 2 cm (3/4 inch) thick. Spread the slices on a baking sheet.

4 Brush the slices lightly with olive oil (about 30-45 ml/2-3 tbsp) and sprinkle with 60 g (2 oz) grated Parmesan cheese. Bake about 5 minutes.
5 Stir the pesto sauce into the hot soup, ladle into warmed bowls, and float a croûte on each serving. Pass remaining croûtes separately. Omit the grated Parmesan cheese for sprinkling.

BORSCHT WITH PIROSHKI

🍽 SERVES 8-10   🥣 WORK TIME 50-55 MINUTES*   ♨ COOKING TIME 1-1¼ HOURS

EQUIPMENT

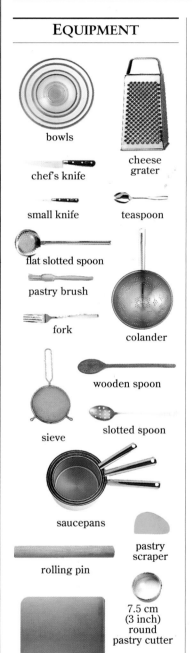

bowls

cheese grater

chef's knife

small knife

teaspoon

flat slotted spoon

pastry brush

fork

colander

wooden spoon

sieve

slotted spoon

saucepans

pastry scraper

rolling pin

7.5 cm (3 inch) round pastry cutter

baking sheet

plate

chopping board

Borscht is the classic soup of Eastern Europe and "piroshki", little savoury turnovers, are the traditional accompaniment.

* plus 45 minutes chilling time

INGREDIENTS

white cabbage

carrots

tomatoes

fresh dill

beetroot

chicken stock

parsley

sugar

flour

red wine vinegar

butter

lemon juice

soured cream

caraway seeds

low-fat curd cheese

eggs

onions

metric	SHOPPING LIST	imperial
1	white cabbage, weighing about 1.4 kg (3 lb)	1
2	carrots, total weight about 150 g (5 oz)	2
3	onions, total weight about 250 g (8 oz)	3
3-4	sprigs of fresh dill	3-4
3-4	sprigs of parsley	3-4
750 g	tomatoes	1½ lb
6	beetroot, total weight about 1 kg (2 lb)	6
	salt and pepper	
60 g	butter	2 oz
2 litres	chicken stock (see box, page 47) or water, more if needed	3¼ pints
5 ml	sugar, or more to taste	1 tsp
	juice of 1 lemon	
30-45 ml	red wine vinegar	2-3 tbsp
60 g	low-fat curd cheese	2 oz
10 ml	caraway seeds	2 tsp
125 ml	soured cream	4 fl oz
For the soured cream dough		
175 g	plain flour	6 oz
1	egg	1
60 g	unsalted butter	2 oz
30 ml	soured cream	2 tbsp
1	egg for glaze	1

ORDER OF WORK

1 **PREPARE THE VEGETABLES**

2 **MAKE THE SOURED CREAM DOUGH**

3 **MAKE THE BORSCHT**

4 **FILL AND BAKE THE PIROSHKI**

1 PREPARE THE VEGETABLES

1 Trim the cabbage, discard any wilted leaves, and cut in half. Cut a wedge around the core in each half and remove. Set the cabbage halves cut side down and finely shred. Discard any thick ribs. Set aside 60 g (2 oz) of the shredded cabbage for the piroshki.

Reserve cabbage for stuffing piroshki

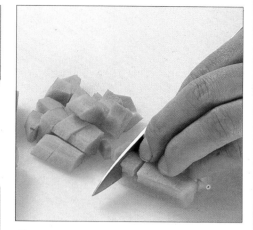

2 Peel the carrots and trim off the ends. Cut each carrot into 4 pieces. Cut each piece lengthwise into 5 mm (¼ inch slices). Stack the slices and cut each stack into 4-6 strips. Gather the strips together into a pile and cut across them.

3 Peel the onions, leaving a little of the root attached, and cut them in half. Slice each half horizontally towards the root, leaving the slices attached at the root end, and then slice vertically, again leaving the root end uncut. Finally, cut across to make dice.

4 Strip the dill and parsley leaves from the stalks and pile them on the chopping board. With the chef's knife, finely chop the leaves.

5 Cut the cores from the tomatoes and score an "x" on the base of each with the tip of a knife. Immerse them in a saucepan of boiling water until the skin starts to split, 8-15 seconds depending on their ripeness. Using the slotted spoon, transfer them at once to a bowl of cold water. When cold, peel off the skin. Cut the tomatoes crosswise in half and squeeze out the seeds, then coarsely chop each half.

Let tomatoes cool before handling

Hot water makes tomato skins split

6 Trim and scrub the beetroot. Bring to a boil in a pan half-filled with salted water. Cook until tender when tested with tip of the small knife, about 30 minutes. Meanwhile, make the soured cream dough.

! TAKE CARE !
Never peel beetroot before cooking because they "bleed".

7 Drain the beetroot. When cool enough to handle, peel off the skin. Grate onto the plate.

2 MAKE THE SOURED CREAM DOUGH

1 Sift the flour onto a work surface and make a well in the centre. Put the egg and 2.5 ml (½ tsp) salt in the well. Using the rolling pin, pound the butter to soften it slightly and add it to the well, then add the soured cream.

2 With your fingertips, work together the egg, salt, butter, and soured cream in the well until the ingredients are thoroughly mixed.

3 Draw in the flour with the pastry scraper. With your fingers, work the flour into the other ingredients until coarse crumbs form. Press the dough into a ball.

ANNE SAYS
"If the dough is very dry, sprinkle it with 15-30 ml (1-2 tbsp) water."

4 Lightly flour the work surface, then blend the dough by pushing it away from you with the heel of your hand. Gather it up with the pastry scraper and continue to blend until it is very smooth and peels away from the work surface in one piece, 1-2 minutes.

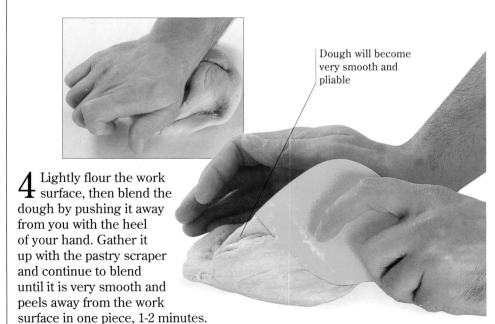

Dough will become very smooth and pliable

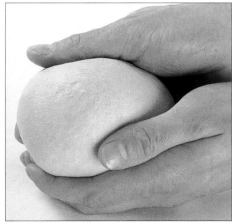

5 Shape the soured cream dough into a ball, wrap it tightly, and chill until firm, about 30 minutes.

3 MAKE THE BORSCHT

1 Melt the butter in a large saucepan. Add the chopped carrots and diced onions and cook, stirring, until soft but not brown, 3-5 minutes. Set aside one quarter of the sautéed vegetables for the piroshki filling.

2 Add the cabbage, beetroot, tomatoes, stock, salt, pepper, and sugar to taste to the saucepan and bring to a boil. Simmer 45-60 minutes. Taste for seasoning and add more stock if too thick. Set aside while you fill and bake the piroshki.

3 Just before serving, reheat the borscht if necessary. Stir in the chopped herbs, lemon juice, and red wine vinegar, and taste for seasoning.

HOW TO MAKE CHICKEN STOCK

Chicken stock is an indispensable ingredient in many sauces and soups. It keeps well up to 3 days, covered, in the refrigerator and it also freezes well. Stock is often reduced to concentrate it, so salt and pepper are not added while it is cooking.

🍽 MAKES 2 LITRES (3¼ PINTS)

🥄 WORK TIME 15 MINUTES

🍲 COOKING TIME UP TO 3 HOURS

SHOPPING LIST

1 kg	raw chicken backs and necks or 1 whole boiling fowl	2-2½ lb
1	onion	1
1	carrot	1
1	celery stick	1
1	bouquet garni made with 5-6 parsley stalks, 2-3 fresh thyme sprigs, and 1 bay leaf	1
2.5-5 ml	peppercorns	½-1 tsp
2 litres	water, more if needed	3¼ pints

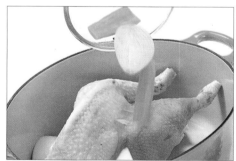

1 Put the chicken in a large pan. Peel and quarter the onion and carrot; quarter the celery. Add to the pan with the bouquet garni and peppercorns.

2 Add water just to cover the ingredients. Bring to a boil and simmer up to 3 hours, skimming the stock occasionally.

3 If using a boiling fowl, remove it when the thigh is tender when pierced with a skewer, 1¼-1¾ hours. The meat can then be used in a recipe calling for cooked chicken.

Strain to remove flavouring ingredients

4 Using a ladle, strain stock into a large bowl.

4 FILL AND BAKE THE PIROSHKI

1 Make the filling: put the reserved shredded cabbage in a bowl. Cover it generously with boiling water and leave 2 minutes. Drain, rinse with cold water, and drain again thoroughly, squeezing out excess water if necessary. Coarsely chop it.

2 Stir the chopped cabbage, curd cheese, and caraway seeds into the reserved carrots and onions. Season with salt and pepper.

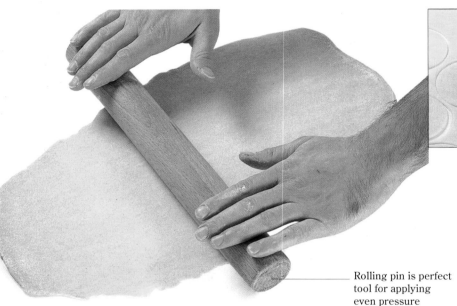

Rolling pin is perfect tool for applying even pressure

3 Lightly flour the work surface. Roll out the soured cream dough about 3 mm (⅛ inch) thick. Cut out rounds from the dough with the pastry cutter or a sharp-edged glass.

ANNE SAYS
"You should have 25-30 rounds. If necessary, roll out the scraps and cut out additional rounds."

Push filling from spoon with finger or another spoon

4 To make the egg glaze, lightly beat the egg with 2.5 ml (½ tsp) salt.

5 Using the teaspoon put a spoonful of filling in the centre of each dough round. Brush the edge of each round with a little egg glaze.

! TAKE CARE !
Do not overfill piroshki or they will burst during cooking.

6 Take one dough round in your fingers, lift the dough to meet on top of the filling, and pinch the edges together to seal. Transfer the piroshki to the baking sheet and brush with the egg glaze. Chill 15 minutes. Heat the oven to 200°C (400°F, Gas 6).

Piroshki should be evenly browned

7 Bake the piroshki in the heated oven until golden brown, 15-18 minutes. Let them cool slightly while you finish the borscht.

Piroshki have tempting golden brown glaze when cooked

🍽 TO SERVE
Pour the soup into a warmed tureen and top with the soured cream. Pass the piroshki separately.

Soured cream is stirred into borscht before serving to add richness

Piroshki are stuffed with cheese and vegetable mixture

V A R I A T I O N

RUSTIC BORSCHT
This hearty variation of Borscht with Piroshki includes beef and its stock.

1 Put a piece of beef shin with bone (weighing about 1.4 kg/3 lb) in a large saucepan and add plenty of water to cover and a little salt. Bring to a boil, then simmer the beef, skimming occasionally, until very tender, 3-4 hours.

2 Prepare the borscht as directed in the main recipe, using a small cabbage (weighing about 1 kg/2 lb) and 2 onions, omitting the tomatoes, and using the beef and its liquid instead of chicken stock.

3 Meanwhile, peel, deseed, and finely chop 1 tomato. Make the piroshki as directed, adding the chopped tomato to the filling.

4 Remove the beef from the borscht. Shred the beef using 2 forks and return it to the soup, discarding the bone. Flavour the borscht with lemon juice and red wine vinegar and serve in individual bowls, topped with the soured cream and chopped herbs.

— GETTING AHEAD —
The borscht can be prepared and kept, covered, in the refrigerator 2-3 days; the flavour improves on standing. It can also be frozen. The piroshki can be baked up to 24 hours ahead and kept in an airtight container, or can be frozen. Reheat in a 180°C (350°F, Gas 4) oven 10 minutes.

PUMPKIN STEW

 SERVES 6   WORK TIME 50-60 MINUTES   COOKING TIME 2¹/₂-3 HOURS

EQUIPMENT

chef's knife

vegetable peeler

small knife

food processor*

lemon squeezer

large metal spoon

wooden spoon

rubber spatula

large baking dish**

colander

bowls

slotted spoon

saucepan

ladle

heatproof casserole

*blender can also be used
**roasting tin can also be used

Stews suggest hearty meals and this one is no exception. A bright orange pumpkin is hollowed out, and its flesh cooked with leeks, tomatoes, and turnips. The stew is then returned to the pumpkin shell for an attractive presentation.

metric	SHOPPING LIST	imperial
1	pumpkin, weighing about 5 kg (12 lb)	1
2 litres	boiling water	3¹/₄ pints
3	medium leeks	3
2	celery sticks	2
2	garlic cloves	2
4	tomatoes, total weight about 500 g (1 lb)	4
175 g	bacon	6 oz
3-5	sprigs of fresh thyme	3-5
1	butternut squash, weighing about 750 g (1¹/₂ lb)	1
1	celeriac, weighing about 750 g (1¹/₂ lb)	1
	juice of ¹/₂ lemon	
5	turnips, total weight about 500 g (1 lb)	5
1	medium courgette	1
125 g	butter	4 oz
30 g	plain flour	1 oz
500 ml	chicken stock, more if needed	16 fl oz
	salt and pepper	
	cayenne	
	sage scones (see box, page 54), for serving (optional)	

INGREDIENTS

pumpkin

celeriac

butter

courgette

leeks

lemon juice

butternut squash

bacon

celery sticks

plain flour

chicken stock

turnips

fresh thyme

tomatoes garlic cloves cayenne

ORDER OF WORK

1 PREPARE THE PUMPKIN SHELL

2 PREPARE THE INGREDIENTS FOR THE STEW

3 MAKE THE STEW

1 PREPARE THE PUMPKIN SHELL

1 Heat the oven to 170°C (325°F, Gas 3). Cut around the stalk end of the pumpkin at an angle and pull off the round "lid". Set the lid aside.

2 Scoop out the seeds with all the fibrous threads and discard them.

ANNE SAYS
"Your hands are the best tools for this."

3 Put the pumpkin in the baking dish. Pour enough boiling water into the pumpkin to fill it. Replace the stalk end and bake until the flesh is just tender, 1½-2 hours.

4 Ladle out and discard the cooking water. With the large spoon, scoop out the flesh without piercing the shell of the pumpkin; the shell should be about 1 cm (½ inch) thick. Set the shell aside and cut the flesh into chunks.

Use ladle to remove water from hot pumpkin

5 Purée the pumpkin chunks in the food processor until smooth.

ANNE SAYS
"You may have to do this in several batches."

2 PREPARE THE INGREDIENTS FOR THE STEW

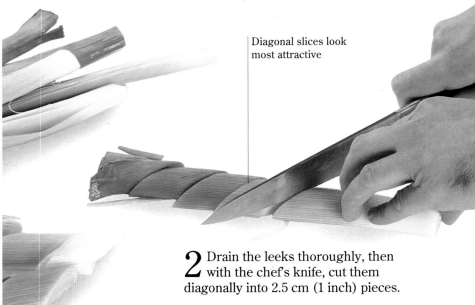

Diagonal slices look most attractive

1 Trim the leeks, discarding the roots and the tough green tops. Slit the leeks lengthwise, put them in the colander, and wash them thoroughly under running water.

2 Drain the leeks thoroughly, then with the chef's knife, cut them diagonally into 2.5 cm (1 inch) pieces.

3 Peel the strings from the celery with the vegetable peeler, then cut the sticks into 1 cm (1/2 inch) slices.

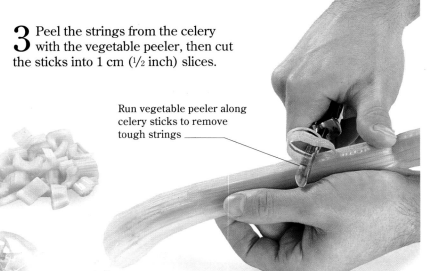

Run vegetable peeler along celery sticks to remove tough strings

4 Set the flat side of the chef's knife on top of each garlic clove and strike it with your fist. Discard the skin and finely chop the garlic.

5 Cut the cores from the tomatoes and score an "x" on the base of each with the tip of the small knife. Immerse them in a pan of boiling water until the skin starts to split. Transfer them at once to a bowl of cold water. When cold, peel off the skin. Cut crosswise in half and squeeze out the seeds, then cut each half into quarters.

6 Cut the bacon crosswise into wide strips. For quick cutting, stack the bacon rashers.

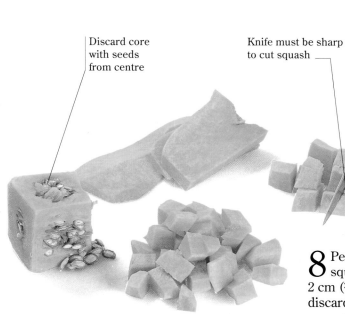

Discard core with seeds from centre

Knife must be sharp to cut squash

7 Strip the thyme leaves from the stalks and pile them on the chopping board. With the chef's knife, finely chop the leaves.

8 Peel the butternut squash and cut it into 2 cm (³/₄ inch) cubes, discarding the seeds.

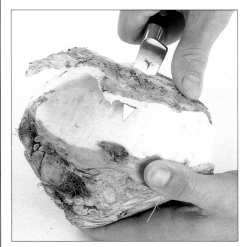

9 Peel the celeriac with the small knife. Square off the sides and cut vertically into 2.5 cm (1 inch) slices.

10 Stack the slices and cut them into 2.5 cm (1 inch) strips. Gather the strips together and cut across into 2.5 cm (1 inch) cubes. Put the cubes of celeriac in a large bowl of water acidulated with the lemon juice, so the cubes do not become brown.

11 Peel the turnips with the vegetable peeler and cut into cubes as for the celeriac.

Remove all green when peeling

12 Trim the courgette and cut into cubes as for the celeriac.

Set slices flat-side down when cutting cubes

SAGE SCONES

🍽 MAKES ABOUT 6

🥣 WORK TIME 30 MINUTES

🍲 COOKING TIME 12-15 MINUTES

SHOPPING LIST

	butter and flour for baking sheet	
8-12	large fresh sage leaves	8-12
250 g	plain flour	8 oz
5 ml	bicarbonate of soda	1 tsp
15 ml	baking powder	1 tbsp
2.5 ml	salt	1/2 tsp
60 g	vegetable shortening or unsalted butter	2 oz
175 ml	milk, more if needed	6 fl oz
5 ml	cream of tartar	1 tsp

1 Heat the oven to 220°C (425°F, Gas 7). Butter and flour a baking sheet. Put the fresh sage leaves in piles of about 4 leaves on a chopping board and chop them with a chef's knife.

2 Sift the flour into a bowl with the bicarbonate of soda, baking powder, and salt; make a well in the centre. Add the shortening and finely cut using 2 round-bladed knives.

3 Rub the mixture with your fingertips until it forms fine crumbs, lifting and crumbling to aerate it. Make a well in the centre and add the chopped sage.

Mix lightly with knife so crumbs form

4 Mix the milk and cream of tartar together and add to the well. Toss quickly to form crumbs. Do not overmix or the scones will be heavy.

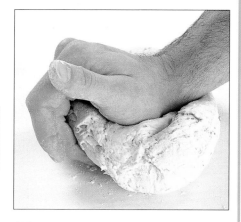

5 Turn the scone dough onto a floured surface and knead lightly for a few seconds – the dough should remain quite rough.

6 Pat the dough out to 2 cm (3/4 inch) thick. Cut out rounds with a 6 cm (2 1/2 inch) round pastry cutter, then pat out the trimmings and cut additional rounds, for a total of 6. Transfer each round to the prepared baking sheet as it is cut.

7 Bake in the heated oven until lightly browned, 12-15 minutes. Transfer to a wire rack to cool slightly before serving.

3 MAKE THE STEW

1 Heat the butter in the casserole, add the bacon, and cook, stirring, until lightly browned, 3-5 minutes. Add the leeks and garlic and soften over low heat, stirring occasionally, 3-5 minutes. Add the flour and cook, stirring, until foaming, 1-2 minutes.

2 Stir in the stock and pumpkin purée. Drain the celeriac and add it to the pot with salt, pepper, and cayenne to taste. Bring to a boil and simmer 20 minutes. Add the celery slices and cubed turnips and simmer 20 minutes longer.

3 Add the squash and courgette cubes, the tomatoes, and thyme and simmer 10 minutes. Taste for seasoning.

Tender vegetables are added last

🍴 TO SERVE

Ladle the stew into the pumpkin shell set on a serving plate. Warm sage scones can be served on the side.

Pumpkin shell is impressive serving container for stew

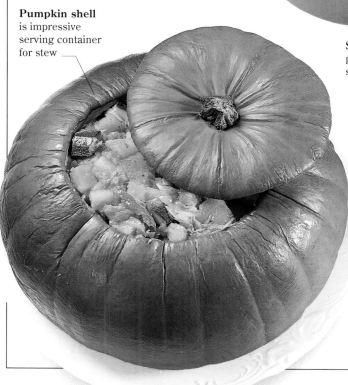

Sage scones make pumpkin stew a substantial meal

PUMPKIN STEW WITH ONION TOPPING

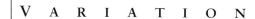

Here the pumpkin stew is served in individual bowls with a topping of fried onions and bacon.

1 Prepare the pumpkin purée as directed; discard the pumpkin shell.
2 Prepare the vegetables and bacon as directed, increasing the quantity of bacon to 275 g (9 oz).
3 After browning the bacon, remove and reserve one-third for the topping. Continue making the stew as directed.
4 Peel 3 medium onions and cut them vertically into thin slices to produce rings. Toss to coat them in 30 ml (2 tbsp) flour seasoned with salt and pepper. Heat 30 ml (2 tbsp) oil in a frying pan and cook the onions, stirring, until browned, 2-3 minutes. Cook the onions in batches if necessary to ensure they will brown nicely. Transfer to paper towels to drain.
5 Ladle the stew into individual bowls, sprinkle with the reserved bacon and browned onions, and decorate the stew with flat-leaved parsley sprigs.

GETTING AHEAD

The pumpkin stew can be made up to 2 days in advance and refrigerated. Reheat it on top of the stove and transfer it to the pumpkin shell just before serving.

MEDITERRANEAN VEGETABLE PLATTER WITH GARLIC SAUCE

Grand Aïoli

🍽 SERVES 8   🥣 WORK TIME 50-60 MINUTES   🍲 COOKING TIME 65-70 MINUTES

EQUIPMENT

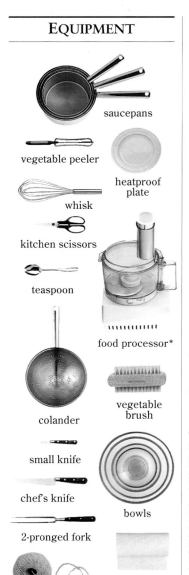

saucepans

vegetable peeler

heatproof plate

whisk

kitchen scissors

teaspoon

food processor*

colander

vegetable brush

small knife

chef's knife

bowls

2-pronged fork

kitchen string

paper towels

serrated knife

*blender can also be used

For "le grand aïoli" a plethora of cold cooked Provençal vegetables are served on a platter, accompanied by a zesty garlic-herb sauce. In Marseille, this dish is traditionally served on Ash Wednesday, and ingredients such as squid, salt cod, or snails may be added.

GETTING AHEAD

The eggs can be boiled and the sauce made up to 2 days ahead and refrigerated. If you like, cook the vegetables up to 6 hours ahead and keep at room temperature.

metric	SHOPPING LIST	imperial
8	eggs	8
8	baby or medium globe artichokes	8
1	lemon	1
500 g	baby or medium carrots	1 lb
4	fennel bulbs	4
500 g	new potatoes	1 lb
500 g	asparagus	1 lb
For the garlic-herb sauce		
2	eggs	2
5-7	sprigs of fresh herbs such as tarragon and parsley	5-7
22.5 ml	butter	1½ tbsp
22.5 ml	plain flour	1½ tbsp
125 ml	boiling water	4 fl oz
4	garlic cloves, or to taste	4
60 ml	olive oil	4 tbsp
	salt and pepper	

INGREDIENTS

globe artichokes

fennel bulbs

olive oil

new potatoes

lemon

fresh herbs

carrots

asparagus

eggs

garlic cloves

butter

plain flour

ORDER OF WORK

1   MAKE THE GARLIC-HERB SAUCE

2   PREPARE AND COOK THE ARTICHOKES

3   PREPARE AND COOK THE CARROTS, FENNEL, AND POTATOES

4   PREPARE AND COOK THE ASPARAGUS

1 MAKE THE GARLIC-HERB SAUCE

Put eggs in cold water after cooking to help loosen shell

1 Put all 10 eggs in a pan of cold water, bring to a boil, and simmer 10 minutes. Drain the eggs.

2 Transfer to a bowl of cold water, and let cool. Tap the eggs to crack, then peel. Rinse with cold water. Set 8 eggs aside in cold water.

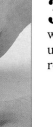

3 Cut the remaining 2 eggs in half and separate the yolks. Discard the whites or set them aside for another use. Strip herb leaves from stalks, reserving a few sprigs for decoration.

4 Melt the butter in a small saucepan. Whisk in the flour and cook until foaming, about 1 minute.

5 Remove from the heat and whisk in the boiling water. Return to a medium heat and cook, stirring, until the sauce reaches a boil and thickens.

! TAKE CARE !
Whisk constantly to ensure the mixture is smooth.

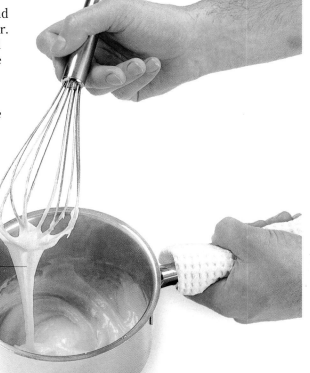

Sauce should be thick enough to coat whisk wires

6 Transfer the sauce to the food processor and add the hard-boiled egg yolks, peeled garlic cloves, and herb leaves. Purée until smooth. With the blades turning, gradually pour in the olive oil, so the sauce becomes creamy. Taste for seasoning, then transfer to a serving bowl.

2 PREPARE AND COOK THE ARTICHOKES

ANNE SAYS
"If the leaves are very tender, rip off the purple-green tops, one at a time, until only a small core of leaves remains in the centre. Then, cut off the tips of these leaves."

1 If using medium globe artichokes, prepare the bottoms (see box, below). If using baby artichokes, trim the stalks, leaving about 5 cm (2 inches). Pull off 2-3 rows of the tough, green, lower leaves. The remaining leaves should be tender.

Rub artichokes with lemon juice to prevent discoloration

2 With the serrated knife, cut off the cone-shaped top of each baby artichoke, but leave the stalk attached to the base. Cut the lemon in half and rub the cut or torn surfaces of each artichoke as it is prepared.

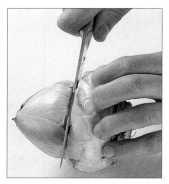

3 With the small knife, peel the stalk of each baby artichoke and trim the base of the stalk so it is smooth.

HOW TO PREPARE GLOBE ARTICHOKE BOTTOMS

 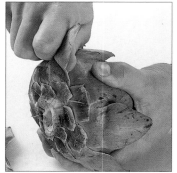 (image) (image)

1 Snap the stalk from a globe artichoke so that the fibres are pulled out with the stalk.

2 Snap off the largest bottom leaves of the artichoke with your hands.

3 Using a very sharp knife, cut off all large bottom leaves, leaving a cone of soft small leaves in the centre.

4 Cut off the soft cone of leaves; discard, leaving only the choke behind.

5 Trim the bottom of any remaining dark green parts, then trim to an even shape, slightly flattened at the base with the top edge bevelled. Rub well with a cut lemon to prevent discoloration. Immerse the artichoke bottom in a bowl of water, acidulated with the juice of ½ lemon, and set aside until ready to cook.

4 Cut very small baby artichokes in half and larger baby ones into quarters. Rub all the cut or torn surfaces of the artichoke pieces with the cut lemon again.

5 Bring a saucepan of water to a boil. Add salt, then the baby artichokes or artichoke bottoms and weigh them down with the heatproof plate so they are submerged. Simmer until tender, 20-25 minutes for baby artichokes or 15-20 minutes for artichoke bottoms.

6 Drain the artichokes in the colander and let cool to tepid. With the teaspoon, scoop out the chokes, removing also tough inner purple leaves from baby artichokes. Cut artichoke bottoms into quarters.

3 PREPARE AND COOK THE CARROTS, FENNEL, AND POTATOES

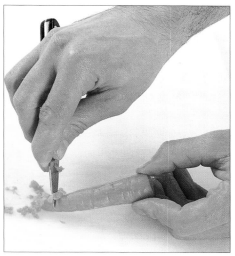

1 If the baby carrots have green tops, trim them, leaving about 5 mm (¼ inch) of green. Scrape the carrots with the small knife to remove the thin skin. If using medium carrots, peel them, then quarter them lengthwise.

ANNE SAYS
"Use a vegetable peeler only if carrots are mature, with a thick skin."

2 Rinse the carrots, put them in a saucepan of cold water, add salt, and bring to a boil. Simmer until just tender, 8-10 minutes. Test with the tip of the small knife. Drain the carrots in the colander, rinse with cold water, and drain again thoroughly.

3 Trim the tops and bases of the fennel bulbs to remove stalks and any dry ends. Discard any tough outer pieces.

Cut off any stalk from fennel bulb

Trim any dry ends from tops of bulbs

4 Cut each fennel bulb lengthwise into quarters. Bring a saucepan of water to a boil, add salt, then the fennel, and simmer until just tender, 12-15 minutes. Drain the fennel in the colander, rinse with cold water, and drain again thoroughly.

5 Rinse the potatoes, scrubbing them gently to remove any dirt. Cut larger potatoes in half.

ANNE SAYS
"So that the potatoes cook in the same time, they should be of uniform size."

6 Put the potatoes in a saucepan of cold water, add salt, and bring to a boil. Simmer until they are just tender, 12-15 minutes. Drain the potatoes in the colander, rinse with cold water, and drain again thoroughly.

4 PREPARE AND COOK THE ASPARAGUS

1 Using the vegetable peeler, strip away the tough, outer skin at the bottom of each asparagus stalk. Trim off woody ends, if necessary. If the asparagus is young and the spears slender, they do not need peeling.

Work from tip of asparagus spear towards base

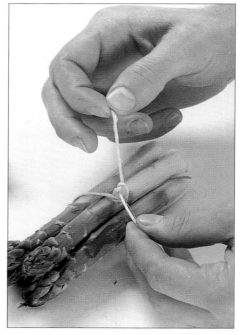

2 With the kitchen string, tie the asparagus into bundles of 5-7 spears each. Bring a shallow pan of water to a boil, add salt, then the asparagus bundles and simmer until just tender, 5-6 minutes.

ANNE SAYS
"Use a shallow, wide pan so that the asparagus can lie flat."

3 Using the 2-pronged fork, transfer the asparagus bundles to the colander, rinse with cold water, and drain on paper towels.

Lift asparagus into colander carefully so spears do not break

VARIATION

VEGETABLE SALAD WITH TAHINI DRESSING

In this variation of Grand Aïoli, the same vegetables are served with a Middle Eastern sauce. Tahini is available from speciality food shops.

1 Prepare and cook the vegetables, and hard-boil and prepare 8 eggs, as directed in the main recipe.

2 To make the tahini dressing: purée 2 garlic cloves in a food processor or blender. Add 125 ml (4 fl oz) tahini paste with the juice of 1 lemon (about 60 ml/4 tbsp) and a generous pinch of salt. Purée until the mixture is smooth, then add water, a little at a time, until the sauce reaches the consistency of soured cream.

3 Arrange the vegetables on individual plates with 2 egg halves each and the tahini sauce in small bowls in the centre. Accompany with toasted wedges of pita bread, if you like.

🍴 **TO SERVE**

Drain and dry the remaining hard-boiled eggs and cut them in half. Arrange the vegetables in sections on a large serving platter. Add the eggs. Decorate with the reserved herb sprigs and serve at room temperature with the bowl of garlic-herb sauce.

Garlic-herb sauce can be as garlicky as you like, according to how many garlic cloves are used

Globe artichokes and bulb fennel are typical Provençal vegetables

STUFFED VEGETABLE TRIO WITH WALNUT-GARLIC SAUCE

🍽 SERVES 4 🥣 WORK TIME 40-45 MINUTES* 🍲 BAKING TIME 15-20 MINUTES

EQUIPMENT

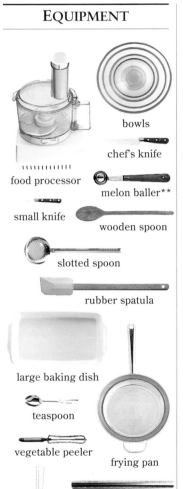

bowls

chef's knife

food processor

melon baller**

small knife

wooden spoon

slotted spoon

rubber spatula

large baking dish

teaspoon

vegetable peeler

frying pan

aluminium foil

large saucepan with lid

pastry brush

paper towels

metal spoon

colander

**teaspoon can also be used

Sweet onions, courgettes, and plump, ripe tomatoes are hollowed out and filled with a grain-based stuffing, then served with a walnut-garlic sauce. Coarse-grained bulghur (cracked wheat) is best for the stuffing, but kasha (buckwheat) can be substituted.

* plus 30 minutes standing time

metric	SHOPPING LIST	imperial
4	large tomatoes, total weight about 625 g (1¹/₄ lb)	4
	salt and pepper	
4	red or Spanish onions, total weight about 750 g (1¹/₂ lb)	4
2	large courgettes, total weight about 500 g (1 lb)	2
250 g	bulghur	8 oz
750 ml	boiling water	1¹/₄ pints
2	celery sticks	2
125 g	fresh shiitake or button mushrooms	4 oz
4	garlic cloves	4
4-6	sprigs of fresh tarragon	4-6
4-6	sprigs of parsley	4-6
45 ml	vegetable oil, more for baking dish and foil	3 tbsp
For the walnut-garlic sauce		
4-6	sprigs of parsley	4-6
4	garlic cloves	4
75 g	walnut halves	2¹/₂ oz
30 ml	cold water	2 tbsp
250 ml	walnut oil	8 fl oz

INGREDIENTS

courgettes

parsley

fresh shiitake mushrooms

fresh tarragon

bulghur

garlic cloves

large tomatoes

large red onions

celery sticks

vegetable oil

walnut halves

walnut oil

ORDER OF WORK

1 **PREPARE THE VEGETABLES**

2 **MAKE THE BULGHUR STUFFING**

3 **STUFF AND BAKE THE VEGETABLES**

4 **MAKE THE WALNUT-GARLIC SAUCE**

1 PREPARE THE VEGETABLES

1 With the small knife, core the tomatoes. If necessary, cut a thin slice from the base of each one so it will sit flat.

2 Cut a slice from the top of each tomato. Scoop out the tomato seeds and flesh with the teaspoon, leaving a 1 cm (1/2 inch) wall of flesh. Scrape the seeds from the scooped-out flesh; reserve the tomato flesh for the stuffing. Season the inside of the tomatoes with salt and pepper, and set them upside-down on paper towels; let drain 30 minutes.

3 Peel the onions with the small knife. Cut a flat slice from the top and a thin slice from the root end of each onion so it will sit flat.

Deep purple-red onions have mild flavour

4 Put the onions in the saucepan and add water to cover. Add salt, put on the lid, and bring to a boil. Simmer until barely tender, 10-15 minutes. Drain the onions on paper towels.

Discard papery skins

5 When cool enough to handle, hollow out the onions, leaving a 1 cm (1/2 inch) wall of onion, by pushing out the core with your fingers. Reserve the onion cores for the stuffing.

6 Trim the courgettes and cut them lengthwise in half. Blanch the courgettes: fill the saucepan with fresh water, bring to a boil, add salt, and then the courgettes. Simmer 3-5 minutes. Drain in the colander and rinse with cold water.

Use melon baller or teaspoon to remove seeds neatly

7 Scoop out and discard the seeds from each of the courgette halves, leaving a 1 cm (1/2 inch) shell of courgette flesh.

2 MAKE THE BULGHUR STUFFING

1 Put the bulghur in a large bowl, pour on the boiling water, cover, and let stand until plump, 30 minutes. Drain off any excess water.

2 Peel the strings from the celery sticks with the vegetable peeler and cut across into thin slices.

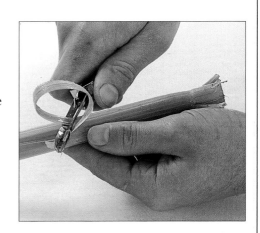

With mushrooms stalk-side down, cut caps into rough quarters

3 Wipe the shiitake mushrooms with a damp paper towel and trim the stalks. Cut the mushrooms into quarters, then chop them.

ANNE SAYS
"You can chop the mushrooms in the food processor, using the pulse button, but do not overwork them or they will form a purée."

4 Set the flat side of the chef's knife on top of the garlic cloves and strike it with your fist. Discard the skin and finely chop the garlic.

5 Chop the reserved onion cores and the tomato flesh. Chop the herbs (see box, right).

HOW TO CHOP HERBS

Parsley, dill, tarragon, rosemary, chives, thyme, and basil are herbs that are usually chopped before being added to other ingredients in a recipe. Delicate herbs such as tarragon and basil are easily bruised, so take care not to chop them too finely.

1 Strip the leaves or sprigs from the stalks of the herbs, then pile the leaves or sprigs on a chopping board.

Fry lightly to retain crunchy texture

Add chopped vegetables to hot oil in pan

6 Heat the oil in the frying pan. Add the celery, garlic, and chopped onion and cook, stirring, until soft but not brown, 2-3 minutes.

7 Add the mushrooms with salt and pepper and continue cooking until all the liquid has evaporated, about 5 minutes longer. Stir in the chopped tomato and cook until the liquid evaporates, about 2 minutes.

2 Cut the leaves or sprigs into small pieces. Holding the tip of the blade against the board and rocking the blade back and forth, continue chopping until the herbs are coarse or fine, as you wish.

ANNE SAYS
"Make sure that your knife is very sharp, otherwise you will bruise the herbs rather than cut them."

8 Add the chopped herbs to the vegetables and taste for seasoning.

9 Mix the sautéed vegetables into the bulghur. Taste for seasoning.

3 STUFF AND BAKE THE VEGETABLES

1 Heat the oven to 190°C (375°F, Gas 5). Oil the baking dish. Spoon the bulghur stuffing into the hollows in the onions, courgettes, and tomatoes. Spread the remaining stuffing over the bottom of the oiled baking dish.

Mound stuffing well in vegetables

2 Arrange the vegetables on the stuffing in the dish. Cover with a piece of oiled foil, transfer to the heated oven, and bake until tender, 15-20 minutes. Meanwhile, make the walnut-garlic sauce.

4 MAKE THE WALNUT-GARLIC SAUCE

1 Strip the parsley sprigs from the stalks and peel the garlic cloves. Purée the walnut halves, peeled garlic, parsley sprigs, and cold water in the food processor or a blender to form a paste. Season with salt and pepper.

Pour in oil slowly

2 With the blade turning, gradually add the walnut oil to the mixture.

3 Scrape down the sides of the processor bowl from time to time with the rubber spatula. When all the walnut oil has been added, taste the sauce for seasoning.

¶◎¶ TO SERVE

Arrange a tomato, an onion, and a courgette half, with extra stuffing from the baking dish, on each of 4 warmed individual plates. Serve the walnut-garlic sauce on the side.

VARIATION
WILD RICE STUFFED VEGETABLE TRIO

Wild rice replaces bulghur as the basis for the filling in this version of stuffed vegetables.

1 Prepare the vegetables as directed.
2 Bring 1.25 litres (2 pints) water to a boil, add salt, then stir in 300 g (10 oz) wild rice. Simmer, covered, until tender, about 40 minutes. Drain. Use in place of the bulghur to make the stuffing.
3 Stuff and bake the vegetables as directed. Serve with walnut-garlic sauce, and decorate with celery leaves.

VARIATION
VEGETABLE TRIO WITH CARROT-RICE STUFFING

Grated carrot is a colourful addition to this trio of stuffed vegetables.

1 Prepare the vegetables as directed.
2 Cook 250 g (8 oz) long-grain white rice in boiling salted water until barely tender, 10-12 minutes. Drain the rice in a colander and rinse with cold running water.
3 Peel and grate 2 medium carrots.
4 Make the stuffing as directed, using the rice in place of the bulghur and stirring in the grated carrot.
5 Stuff and bake the vegetables as directed and serve with the walnut-garlic sauce.

GETTING AHEAD

The vegetables can be prepared 24 hours ahead and kept, covered, in the refrigerator. Reheat them 15 minutes in an oven heated to 180°C (350°F, Gas 4), or serve them at room temperature.

Parsley sprigs are fresh decoration

Sauce is pungent, and perfect with stuffed vegetables

MOSAIC OF VEGETABLES WITH CHICKEN MOUSSE

🍽 SERVES 6-8 🥄 WORK TIME ABOUT 1 HOUR 🍲 COOKING TIME 1½-1¾ HOURS

EQUIPMENT

vegetable peeler

bowls

pastry brush

metal spoon

food processor*

chef's knife

30 x 9 x 7.5 cm
(11½ x 3½ x 3 inch)
terrine mould

whisk

frying pan

saucepans

palette knife

colander

wooden spoon

tea towel

roasting tin

aluminium foil

rubber spatula

metal skewer
*blender can also be used

This nouvelle cuisine mosaic of vegetables, held together with a light chicken mousse, has become a classic. If you're short of time, omit the French beans and double the amount of spinach.

GETTING AHEAD
The mosaic and mustard sauce can be made up to 2 days ahead and refrigerated.

metric	SHOPPING LIST	imperial
500 g	spinach	1 lb
	salt and white pepper	
15 g	softened butter, more for terrine mould	½ oz
	ground nutmeg	
350 g	carrots	12 oz
250 g	French beans	8 oz
For the chicken mousse		
750 g	boneless chicken breasts	1½ lb
1	egg	1
45 g	butter, at room temperature	1½ oz
175 ml	double cream	6 fl oz
For the mustard sauce		
2	eggs	2
20 g	butter	¾ oz
22.5 ml	plain flour	1½ tbsp
125 ml	boiling water	4 fl oz
1	garlic clove	1
45 ml	Dijon mustard	3 tbsp
60 ml	olive oil	4 tbsp

INGREDIENTS

eggs

plain flour

spinach

chicken breasts

butter

double cream

ground nutmeg

Dijon mustard

French beans

garlic clove

carrots

olive oil

ORDER OF WORK

1 LINE THE TERRINE MOULD

2 PREPARE THE VEGETABLES

3 MAKE THE CHICKEN MOUSSE

4 FILL AND BAKE THE TERRINE

5 MAKE THE MUSTARD SAUCE

1 LINE THE TERRINE MOULD

Leave no gaps between spinach leaves

1 Discard the tough ribs and stalks from the spinach leaves, then wash them thoroughly.

2 Bring a large pan of water to a boil, add salt, then the spinach, and blanch 1 minute. Drain in the colander, rinse with cold water, and drain again thoroughly, patting it dry with the tea towel and keeping as many leaves whole as possible.

3 Thoroughly brush the terrine mould with butter. Arrange the whole spinach leaves on the bottom and sides of the mould, allowing about 5 cm (2 inches) of spinach to overhang the edge of the mould.

2 PREPARE THE VEGETABLES

Cut carrot pieces into neat slices

1 Chop the remaining spinach. Heat the butter in a small pan, add the spinach, and sauté, stirring, until the moisture has evaporated, 2-3 minutes. Season with salt, pepper, and a pinch of ground nutmeg.

2 Peel and trim the carrots. Cut across in half, then cut lengthwise into 1 cm (1/2 inch) slices. Put the carrots in a saucepan of cold water, add salt, bring to a boil, and cook until tender, 7-10 minutes. Drain thoroughly.

3 Snap the ends from the French beans. Bring a pan of salted water to a boil, add the French beans, and cook until just tender, 5-7 minutes. Drain them, rinse with cold water, and drain again thoroughly. Sprinkle all the vegetables with salt and pepper.

3 MAKE THE CHICKEN MOUSSE

Add egg through feed tube

Fry mixture until browned and cooked

1 Cut the chicken breasts into chunks, discarding any skin. Put the chunks in the food processor and purée until smooth. Add the egg and then the softened butter to the chicken and purée to combine.

2 Transfer the mixture to a bowl and set it in a larger bowl of iced water. Beat with the wooden spoon until the mixture is chilled. Using the rubber spatula, beat in the double cream a little at a time. Season with salt, white pepper, and a pinch of nutmeg.

ANNE SAYS
"It's preferable to use white pepper so there will be no specks in the mousse, but black pepper can be used."

3 To test the seasoning of the chicken mixture, fry a little in the frying pan and then taste it. Adjust the seasoning of the remaining mixture, if necessary.

4 FILL AND BAKE THE TERRINE

Lay carrot slices neatly on mousse to make solid layer

1 Heat the oven to 180°C (350°F, Gas 4). Spread about one-sixth of the chicken mousse mixture evenly over the spinach leaves on the bottom of the mould, using the palette knife.

2 Arrange one-quarter of the carrot slices lengthwise on top and cover them with a thin layer of mousse.

3 Add another layer of carrot slices and then mousse. Arrange half of the beans on top of the mousse.

4 Cover the beans with a thin layer of mousse. Spoon the spinach onto the mousse and spread it out into an even layer.

Fold spinach leaves over mousse to cover completely

5 Top with a layer of mousse, then a layer of beans. Layer the carrots with mousse in between, ending with a final layer of mousse. Fold the overhanging spinach over the top.

Push skewer into centre of mosaic when testing if it is cooked

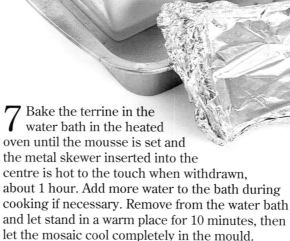

6 Cover the terrine mould with buttered foil and put it in the roasting tin. Pour in boiling water to come more than halfway up the sides of the mould to make a bain-marie (water bath).

7 Bake the terrine in the water bath in the heated oven until the mousse is set and the metal skewer inserted into the centre is hot to the touch when withdrawn, about 1 hour. Add more water to the bath during cooking if necessary. Remove from the water bath and let stand in a warm place for 10 minutes, then let the mosaic cool completely in the mould.

5 MAKE THE MUSTARD SAUCE

1 Half-fill a saucepan with cold water, add the eggs, then bring to a boil, and simmer 10 minutes. Drain the eggs, then transfer to a bowl of cold water and let cool.

Use chef's knife to chop whites finely

2 Tap the eggs to crack the shells, then peel them. Rinse the eggs with cold water. Cut them in half and put the yolks in a bowl. Finely chop the whites.

3 Melt the butter in a small saucepan. Whisk in the flour and cook until foaming, about 1 minute. Remove from the heat and whisk in the boiling water. The sauce will thicken at once. Return it to the heat and cook, stirring, for 1 minute.

ANNE SAYS
"The sauce will thicken as soon as the boiling water is added."

4 Transfer the sauce to the food processor, add the hard-boiled egg yolks, garlic, mustard, salt, and pepper, and purée until smooth.

Keep processor running while adding oil

5 With the blades turning, pour in the olive oil in a thin stream, so the sauce thickens and becomes creamy.

! TAKE CARE !
Do not add the oil too quickly, or the mixture will separate.

6 Pour the sauce into a bowl and stir in the chopped egg whites. Taste the sauce for seasoning. Cover and set the sauce aside.

ANNE SAYS
"The sauce will thicken as it sits."

Fold in egg whites with rubber spatula

🍴 TO SERVE
Set a serving plate, upside-down, on the terrine and invert to turn out the mosaic. Carefully cut it into slices and serve the mustard sauce separately.

Chicken mousse mixture holds vegetables firmly together

MOSAIC OF VEGETABLES WITH CHEESE
A cheese-based mixture holds this vegetable mosaic together, and the sauce is made with red peppers.

1 Prepare and chop all of the spinach. Cut the carrots lengthwise in half, then into thin strips; cook as directed. Prepare and cook the French beans as directed. Grate 250 g (8 oz) Gruyère cheese.
2 Sprinkle 15 ml (1 tbsp) powdered gelatine over 125 ml (4 fl oz) cold water and let stand, about 5 minutes.
3 Whisk together 375 ml (12 fl oz) double cream, 5 egg yolks, salt, pepper, and a pinch of nutmeg. Heat the gelatine until melted. Stir into the cream.
4 Layer the carrots and beans in the terrine, with the spinach in a cylinder shape in the middle, and a little of the grated cheese and the cream mixture between each layer. Do not pack down.
5 Poke the mosaic with a skewer; cover with the remaining cream mixture.
6 Cover and bake in the water bath as directed, 1½-2 hours. Let cool completely, then refrigerate.
7 To make the sauce: peel, core, and deseed 750 g (1½ lb) red peppers, then cut into chunks. Peel, deseed, and chop 500 g (1 lb) tomatoes. Chop 1 garlic clove, 2 spring onions, and a small bunch of basil leaves. Heat 30 ml (2 tbsp) olive oil in a frying pan. Cook all the ingredients, stirring, until thickened, 15-20 minutes. Purée in a food processor until almost smooth. Season.
8 Turn out the mosaic and serve with the cold red pepper sauce.

CABBAGE WITH CHESTNUT AND PORK STUFFING

🍽 SERVES 6　🥣 WORK TIME 35-40 MINUTES　🍲 COOKING TIME 50-60 MINUTES

EQUIPMENT

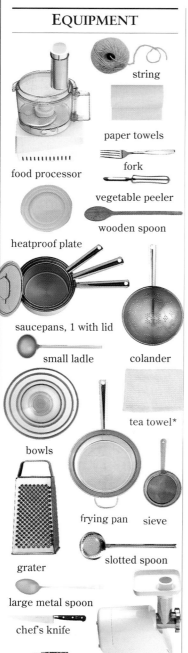

string

paper towels

food processor

fork

vegetable peeler

wooden spoon

heatproof plate

saucepans, 1 with lid

small ladle

colander

tea towel*

bowls

grater

frying pan

sieve

slotted spoon

large metal spoon

chef's knife

small knife　mincer

metal skewer

*muslin can also be used

Stuffed cabbage is an old favourite. Here the leaves are blanched, then reassembled around a richly flavoured stuffing. Served with a tomato-mushroom sauce, it makes a hearty main course.

metric	SHOPPING LIST	imperial
1	head of Savoy cabbage, weighing 1.4 kg (3 lb)	1
	For the chestnut stuffing	
1 kg	fresh chestnuts or 500 g (1 lb) canned or vacuum-packed unsweetened chestnuts	2 lb
125 g	lean boneless pork	4 oz
1	onion	1
1	lemon	1
10-12	sprigs of parsley	10-12
10-12	leaves of fresh sage	10-12
2	celery sticks	2
2	slices of white bread	2
60 g	butter	2 oz
	salt and pepper	
2	eggs	2
	For the tomato and mushroom sauce	
500 g	tomatoes	1 lb
1	small onion	1
125 g	mushrooms	4 oz
1	garlic clove	1
30 ml	vegetable oil	2 tbsp
15 ml	tomato purée	1 tbsp
1	bouquet garni made with 10-12 parsley stalks, 2-3 thyme sprigs, and 1 bay leaf	1
	granulated sugar	

INGREDIENTS

chestnuts　lean pork

Savoy cabbage

lemon

onion

celery sticks

butter　white bread

vegetable oil

bouquet garni

tomato purée

sugar

mushrooms

fresh sage

garlic clove

eggs　tomatoes

parsley

ORDER OF WORK

1 PREPARE THE CABBAGE

2 MAKE THE CHESTNUT STUFFING

3 STUFF AND COOK THE CABBAGE

4 MAKE THE TOMATO AND MUSHROOM SAUCE

1 PREPARE THE CABBAGE

1 Using the small knife, cut the outside leaf from the base of the cabbage stalk and carefully peel the leaf away from the head. Repeat until you have 10 large cabbage leaves. Wash the leaves well in cold water.

2 Bring a large saucepan of water to a boil. Add salt, then immerse the 10 cabbage leaves in the water and blanch 1 minute, just to soften them. With the slotted spoon, transfer the cabbage leaves to a bowl of cold water.

3 Trim the stalk from the cabbage head and cook it in the boiling water, 3-4 minutes. Transfer it to a bowl of cold water. When cool, remove and let drain thoroughly, stalk-end down, in the colander.

Outer leaves have deepest green colour

Use small knife to cut out thick centre rib

4 When the leaves are cool, drain and pat dry with paper towels. Cut out and discard the thick rib at the centre of each large cabbage leaf.

5 Cut the cabbage head in half. Cut a wedge around the core in each piece of cabbage and remove it.

6 Set each half cut-side down on the chopping board and slice it crosswise into thin shreds. Discard any thick ribs. Roll up any loose leaves and cut them crosswise into shreds.

2 MAKE THE CHESTNUT STUFFING

1 If using fresh chestnuts, pierce each one with the point of the small knife. Put them in a pan with water to cover and bring to a boil. Remove a few chestnuts at a time and peel them with the knife while they are still hot.

If chestnuts become difficult to peel, return them to pan of water to reheat

2 Pour the water from the pan, put in the peeled chestnuts, and cover with fresh water. Cover the pan with the lid and simmer until tender, 25-30 minutes. Drain well, then coarsely chop the chestnuts.

ANNE SAYS
"Canned and vacuum-packed chestnuts need not be cooked. Just drain them."

3 Cut the pork into 2-3 pieces and the onion into quarters. Work the pork and onion through the fine blade of the mincer or in the food processor.

4 Grate the zest from the lemon. Strip the parsley leaves from the sprigs and pile them on the chopping board with the sage leaves. With the chef's knife, finely chop the leaves.

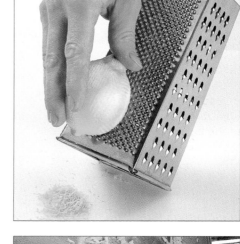

5 Peel the strings from the celery with the vegetable peeler and cut the sticks across into thin slices. Trim and discard the crusts from the bread. Work the bread slices in the food processor, or in a blender, to form crumbs.

Celery slices neatly when strings have been removed

6 Melt the butter in the frying pan, add the shredded cabbage, and cook, stirring occasionally, until tender, 7-10 minutes. Transfer the cabbage to a large bowl, using the slotted spoon.

Add pork mixture all at once

7 Put the minced pork and onion into the frying pan with the celery. Cook, stirring occasionally, until the minced pork is crumbled and brown, 5-7 minutes.

8 Add the breadcrumbs, chestnuts, chopped herbs, lemon zest, salt, and pepper to the shredded cabbage in the bowl. Add the pork mixture and stir well together. Taste for seasoning.

9 Lightly beat the eggs with the fork. Pour the beaten eggs into the stuffing mixture in the bowl and stir well together.

3 STUFF AND COOK THE CABBAGE

1 Line a large bowl with the dampened tea towel. Arrange 9 of the blanched cabbage leaves in an overlapping layer around the inside of the bowl, stalk-ends up. Allow about 5 cm (2 inches) of the leaves to extend above the rim of the bowl. Set the last leaf in the bottom of the bowl.

Arrange leaves to recreate original cabbage-head shape

2 Spoon in the chestnut stuffing, then press it down gently and smooth.

3 Fold the ends of the cabbage leaves over to enclose the chestnut stuffing completely.

4 Gather the ends of the cloth over the top of the cabbage leaves and tie them together with a piece of the string to make a tight ball.

5 Bring a large pan of water to a boil. Immerse the stuffed cabbage "head" in the water and set the heatproof plate on top to weigh it down.

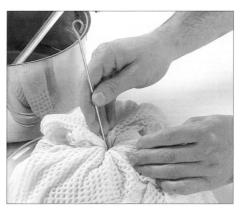

6 Simmer until the skewer inserted in the centre for 30 seconds comes out hot to the touch when removed, 50-60 minutes. Meanwhile, make the tomato and mushroom sauce.

4 MAKE THE TOMATO AND MUSHROOM SAUCE

1 Chop the tomatoes without peeling them. Peel the onion, leaving a little of the root attached, and cut it in half. Slice each half horizontally towards the root, leaving the slices attached at the root end. Slice vertically, again leaving the root end uncut. Cut across to make dice, then chop until very fine.

Tomato skin and seeds will be sieved out later

2 Wipe the mushrooms with a damp paper towel and trim the stalks level with the caps. Set the mushrooms stalk-side down on the chopping board and slice them. Set the flat side of the chef's knife on top of the garlic clove and strike it with your fist. Discard the skin and finely chop the garlic.

3 Heat half of the vegetable oil in the frying pan. Add the chopped onion and cook, stirring with the wooden spoon, until soft, 2-3 minutes.

4 Stir in the tomatoes, tomato purée, garlic, bouquet garni, salt, pepper, and a pinch of sugar and cook, stirring occasionally, until the mixture is fairly thick, 8-10 minutes.

Sieving removes bouquet garni as well as tomato skins and seeds

5 Sieve the tomato mixture into a bowl, pressing down with the ladle to extract all the pulp.

6 Wipe the frying pan, heat the remaining oil, and sauté the mushrooms until tender, without letting them brown. Stir in the tomato sauce and taste for seasoning.

🍴 **TO SERVE**
Lift the stuffed "cabbage" carefully from the pan, drain, and let cool slightly. Unwrap and set it, stalk-side down, on a warm serving plate. Spoon over some of the tomato and mushroom sauce and pass the rest separately. Cut into wedges to serve.

Fresh tomato and mushroom sauce is colourful contrasting accompaniment

Rich stuffing of chestnuts and pork is flavoured with lemon and herbs

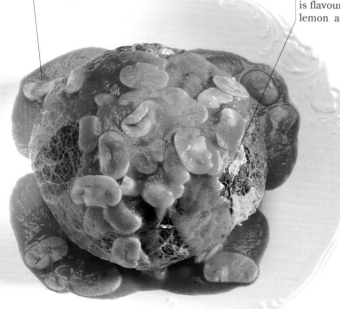

V A R I A T I O N

BABY GREEN CABBAGES STUFFED WITH PORK

Ham and pork fill the centres of these individual stuffed cabbages, served with soured cream or plain yogurt.

1 Prepare the cabbage as directed.
2 Make the stuffing as directed, omitting the chestnuts and using a total of 500 g (1 lb) lean boneless pork.
3 Line 6 small bowls with table napkins or muslin. Add blanched cabbage leaves, using 2 leaves for each bowl.
4 Place 1 slice of ham on top of the cabbage in each bowl. Fill with the stuffing.

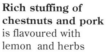

5 Tie up each stuffed cabbage "head" and cook as directed, allowing about 30 minutes.
6 Omit the tomato and mushroom sauce. Serve with soured cream or plain yogurt and decorate with fresh thyme.

GETTING AHEAD

The stuffed cabbage and tomato and mushroom sauce can be cooked 2 days ahead and kept refrigerated. Reheat the cabbage in a covered casserole with a little liquid in an oven heated to 180°C (350°F, Gas 4).

GRATIN OF CHICORY AND HAM

 SERVES 4 WORK TIME 15-20 MINUTES  BAKING TIME 1-1¼ HOURS

EQUIPMENT

saucepans, 1 with lid

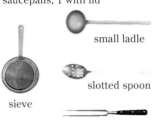
small ladle

slotted spoon

sieve

2-pronged fork

plate

pastry brush

cheese grater

small knife

whisk

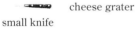

paper towels   flan dish*

aluminium foil

chopping board

* shallow baking dish can also be used

INGREDIENTS

chicory

Gruyère cheese

milk

sliced cooked ham

onion

granulated sugar

ground nutmeg   bay leaf

plain flour

peppercorns   butter

In this simple dish from Belgium, home of chicory, thin slices of cooked ham are wrapped round braised chicory and then baked in a cream sauce sprinkled with cheese.

GETTING AHEAD
The gratin can be assembled up to the baking stage the day before, then covered tightly and refrigerated.

metric	SHOPPING LIST	imperial
	butter for flan dish and foil	
8	medium heads of chicory, total weight about 1 kg (2 lb)	8
5 ml	granulated sugar	1 tsp
	salt and pepper	
45 g	Gruyère cheese	1½ oz
8	thin slices of cooked ham, total weight about 375 g (12 oz)	8
	For the béchamel sauce	
500 ml	milk	16 fl oz
1	slice of onion	1
1	bay leaf	1
6	peppercorns	6
60 g	butter	2 oz
30 g	plain flour	1 oz
	ground nutmeg	

ORDER OF WORK

1 BRAISE CHICORY

2 MAKE THE BÉCHAMEL SAUCE

3 ASSEMBLE AND BAKE THE GRATIN

1 BRAISE CHICORY

1 Heat the oven to 180°C (350°F, Gas 4). Brush the flan dish with butter. Trim the chicory, wipe clean, and discard any wilted leaves.

Fresh chicory is plump and white

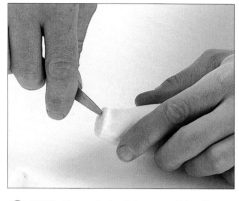

2 With the point of the small knife, hollow each stalk. If the heads of chicory are large, cut them in half.

ANNE SAYS
"This allows the chicory to cook more evenly and removes the parts that may be bitter."

3 Arrange the chicory in the prepared flan dish and sprinkle with the sugar, salt, and pepper. Butter a piece of foil and press it, buttered-side down, on top.

4 Bake the chicory in the heated oven, turning once or twice with the 2-pronged fork, until they are brown and tender, 45-55 minutes. Using the slotted spoon, transfer the chicory to the plate and let cool slightly. Wipe the flan dish.

2 MAKE THE BECHAMEL SAUCE

Onion and herbs flavour milk

1 Scald the milk in a medium saucepan with the onion slice, bay leaf, and peppercorns. Cover the saucepan and let the milk stand in a warm place, 10 minutes.

ANNE SAYS
"For a simple white sauce, bring the milk to a boil omitting the onion slice, bay leaf, and peppercorns."

Straining removes flavouring ingredients

2 Melt the butter in another saucepan over medium heat. Whisk in the flour and cook until foaming, 30-60 seconds.

3 Remove from the heat and let cool slightly, then strain in the hot milk and whisk to mix. Return to the heat and cook, whisking constantly, until the sauce boils and thickens. Season with salt, pepper, and a pinch of nutmeg, and simmer 2 minutes.

! TAKE CARE !
If the sauce forms lumps at any stage, remove from the heat and whisk vigorously. If whisking is not sufficient, strain the sauce.

3 ASSEMBLE AND BAKE THE GRATIN

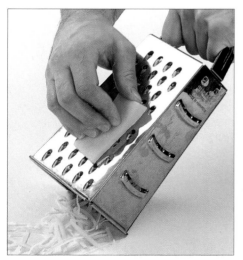

Centre chicory on ham slice to roll up neatly

1 Heat the oven to 200°C (400°F, Gas 6). Butter the flan dish again. Grate the Gruyère cheese and set aside.

2 Lay a slice of ham on the work surface. Set a head of chicory on top and roll the ham slice round the chicory to form a neat cylinder.

3 Repeat with the remaining ham slices and chicory, arranging the cylinders neatly in the prepared dish, folded-side down, to keep them intact.

4 Ladle the béchamel sauce evenly over the chicory and ham cylinders.

5 Sprinkle with the grated cheese. Bake in the heated oven until bubbling and browned, 20-25 minutes. If necessary, heat the grill and grill the gratin until the top is brown. Serve hot from the flan dish.

Gruyère cheese topping is brown and crisp

Chicory heads are wrapped in tasty ham slices

VARIATION

BROCCOLI AND CAULIFLOWER GRATIN

This gratin is flavoured with Parmesan cheese instead of ham.

1 Trim 1-2 heads of broccoli (total weight about 500 g/1 lb) and 1 cauliflower (weighing about 750 g/1½lb). Cut the broccoli and cauliflower florets from the stalks; cut large florets in half.
2 Bring 2 pans of water to a boil. Add salt and the broccoli and cauliflower florets to separate pans. Cook until just tender, 5-10 minutes. Drain thoroughly.
3 Arrange the florets in a buttered shallow baking dish, alternating the colours in a chequer-board pattern.
4 Make the béchamel sauce, adding 125 ml (4 fl oz) extra milk. Remove from the heat and whisk in 20 g (¾ oz) grated Parmesan cheese.
5 Spoon the sauce evenly over the florets and sprinkle with the grated Gruyère cheese. Bake as directed.

VARIATION

INDIVIDUAL GRATINS OF LEEK AND HAM

Leeks replace the heads of chicory in this variation.

1 Trim 1 kg (2 lb) leeks, discarding the roots and tough tops. Cut off and reserve some of the tender green tops. Slit the leeks lengthwise and wash them thoroughly under cold running water in a colander.
2 Put the leeks in a pan of salted water, bring to a boil and cook until tender, 12-20 minutes, depending on their size. Drain them, rinse with cold water, and drain again thoroughly. Cut the leeks into 10 cm (4 inch) lengths.
3 Cut the reserved green leek tops lengthwise in half, then cut lengthwise into thin strips to make julienne. Bring a pan of salted water to a boil; add leek tops and cook until tender, 3-5 minutes. Drain and set aside for garnish.
4 Make the béchamel sauce as directed in the main recipe.
5 Heat the grill. Cut the ham into strips 7.5 cm (3 inches) wide. Wrap the leek pieces in the ham strips so that the leeks show at each end. Arrange 3-4 on individual heatproof plates.
6 Spoon the sauce on top, omitting the grated cheese. Grill the gratins until browned, 3-5 minutes. Sprinkle the green leek julienne on the gratins just before serving.

ARTICHOKES STUFFED WITH MUSHROOMS AND OLIVES

Artichauts à la Barigoule

🍽 SERVES 4   🥣 WORK TIME 50-55 MINUTES   🍲 BAKING TIME 40-45 MINUTES

EQUIPMENT

chef's knife

small knife

metal spoon

teaspoon

ladle

kitchen scissors

wooden spoon

slotted spoon

rubber spatula

heatproof plate

plastic bag

wire rack

frying pan

food processor*

bowls

large flameproof casserole with lid

medium saucepan

kitchen string

*blender can also be used

INGREDIENTS

globe artichokes

Parma ham

anchovy fillets

fresh thyme

mushrooms   onions

fresh basil

butter

black olives

olive oil

spring onions

lemon

ground allspice

red peppers   white bread

tomatoes   garlic cloves

white wine

"A la barigoule" describes a Provençal method of preparing stuffed artichokes. Here, the artichokes are simmered with white wine and served with a rich red pepper sauce.

metric	SHOPPING LIST	imperial
4	globe artichokes, total weight about 1.4 kg (3 lb)	4
1/2	lemon	1/2
	salt and pepper	
250 ml	white wine	8 fl oz
For the mushroom and olive stuffing		
6	garlic cloves	6
3	small onions	3
250 g	mushrooms	8 oz
2-3	sprigs of fresh thyme	2-3
2	anchovy fillets	2
175 g	stoned black olives	6 oz
250 g	Parma ham	8 oz
4	slices of white bread	4
45 g	butter	1 1/2 oz
	ground allspice	
For the red pepper sauce		
750 g	red peppers	1 1/2 lb
500 g	tomatoes	1 lb
1	garlic clove	1
2	spring onions	2
1	small bunch of fresh basil	1
30 ml	olive oil	2 tbsp

ORDER OF WORK

1. **PREPARE THE ARTICHOKES**

2. **MAKE THE STUFFING**

3. **STUFF AND BAKE THE ARTICHOKES**

4. **MAKE THE RED PEPPER SAUCE**

1 PREPARE THE ARTICHOKES

1 Snap the stalk from each artichoke so that the fibres are pulled out with the stalk.

Grip stalk firmly so it snaps sharply

2 Trim the base of each artichoke with the chef's knife so they sit flat, and rub the cut surfaces with the lemon half to prevent discoloration.

3 Trim the outer leaves from all the artichokes with the kitchen scissors to remove the pointed leaf tips.

4 With the chef's knife, cut off about 2 cm (³/₄ inch) from the pointed top of each artichoke. Rub all cut surfaces with lemon.

Keep artichokes submerged in water while they cook so they do not discolour

5 Fill the casserole with water, bring to a boil, and add salt. Remove from heat and add the artichokes. Weigh them down with the heatproof plate or a wet cloth to submerge them. Return to heat and simmer until almost tender and a leaf can be pulled out with a slight tug, 25-30 minutes. Set 1 artichoke on the wire rack to test.

ANNE SAYS
"Make the stuffing while the artichokes are cooking."

6 Lift out the artichokes with the slotted spoon and set them upside-down on the wire rack placed over the tray to drain.

7 When the artichokes are cool enough to handle, remove the inner leaves by twisting them out with your fingers.

When artichoke is fully cooked, choke is easy to remove

8 With the teaspoon, scoop out the choke from each to make a neat cavity for the stuffing.

2 MAKE THE STUFFING

1 Set the flat side of the chef's knife on top of each garlic clove and strike it with your fist. Discard the skin and finely chop the garlic. Peel the onions, leaving a little of the root attached to each, and cut them in half through root and stalk. Slice each half horizontally towards the root, leaving the slices attached at the root end, then slice vertically, again leaving the root end uncut. Cut across the onion to make dice.

Slice just to root each time, so onion holds together

2 Wipe the mushroom caps with a damp paper towel and trim the stalks. Cut the caps into quarters and coarsely chop them in the food processor, using the pulse button. Or, chop with the chef's knife.

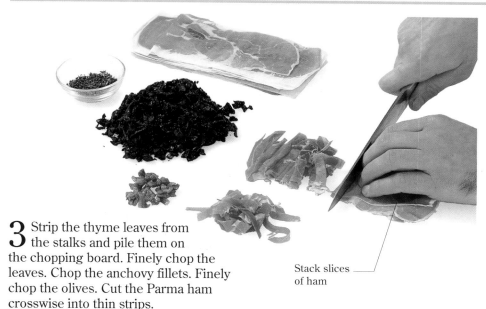

3 Strip the thyme leaves from the stalks and pile them on the chopping board. Finely chop the leaves. Chop the anchovy fillets. Finely chop the olives. Cut the Parma ham crosswise into thin strips.

Stack slices of ham

4 Trim and discard the crusts from the bread. Work the bread slices in the food processor to form crumbs.

5 Melt the butter in the frying pan, add the chopped onions and garlic, and cook, stirring with the wooden spoon, until soft but not brown.

6 Stir in the mushrooms, Parma ham, anchovies, and olives, then remove the pan from the heat. Add the breadcrumbs, chopped thyme, and a large pinch of allspice and mix thoroughly. Season to taste with pepper.

3 STUFF AND BAKE THE ARTICHOKES

1 Heat the oven to 180°C (350°F, Gas 4). Fill the cavity in the centre of each artichoke with stuffing.

Mound stuffing well in artichokes

2 Tie a piece of kitchen string around each of the stuffed artichokes to hold the leaves together.

Wine will give flavour but alcohol is boiled away

String holds shape of artichokes as they simmer

3 Put the artichokes in the casserole and pour in the wine. Put the casserole over high heat, bring the wine to a boil, and boil until reduced by half, about 5 minutes. Pour in enough water to half cover the artichokes and add salt and pepper. Bring back to a boil and cover with the lid.

ANNE SAYS
"The casserole should be deep enough to hold the artichokes and large enough for them to fit snugly."

4 Transfer to the oven. Bake, basting occasionally, until tender and a central leaf can be pulled out easily, 40-50 minutes. Meanwhile, make the red pepper sauce.

ANNE SAYS
"Add more water during cooking if necessary to keep the artichokes moist."

4 MAKE THE RED PEPPER SAUCE

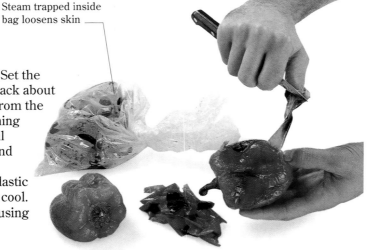

Steam trapped inside bag loosens skin

1 Heat the grill. Set the peppers on a rack about 10 cm (4 inches) from the heat and grill, turning once or twice, until the skin is black and blistered. Put the peppers into the plastic bag, close, and let cool. Peel the peppers, using the small knife.

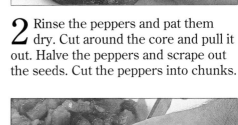

2 Rinse the peppers and pat them dry. Cut around the core and pull it out. Halve the peppers and scrape out the seeds. Cut the peppers into chunks.

3 Score an "x" on the base of each tomato. Immerse them in boiling water until the skin starts to split. Transfer to cold water, then peel.

4 Cut the tomatoes in half and squeeze out the seeds. Chop the tomato halves.

5 Chop the garlic. Chop the spring onions. Strip the basil leaves from the stalks, reserving 4 sprigs for garnish, and finely chop the leaves.

6 Heat the olive oil in the frying pan. Add the peppers, tomatoes, garlic, spring onions, and basil and cook, stirring occasionally, until thickened, 15-20 minutes.

7 Put the sauce in the food processor and purée until still slightly chunky in texture. Season the sauce to taste with salt and pepper.

Artichoke leaves can be pulled out one by one and dipped in red pepper sauce before tender bases are eaten

🍴🍽️ **TO SERVE**

Discard the strings from the artichokes and put the artichokes on individual plates. Spoon some red pepper sauce around the base of each artichoke, garnish with a basil sprig, and pass the remaining sauce separately.

Basil sprig garnish echoes flavouring of red pepper sauce

V A R I A T I O N

ARTICHOKES WITH HERB-BUTTER SAUCE

Artichokes, complemented by a herb-butter sauce, make an excellent first course.

1 Prepare the artichokes as directed, cooking them for 35-45 minutes, until a central leaf can be pulled out easily. Drain upside-down and let cool slightly.
2 Meanwhile, make the sauce: finely chop 2 shallots. Boil with 45 ml (3 tbsp) each white wine vinegar and white wine, until reduced to a glaze. Add 15 ml (1 tbsp) double cream and boil again to a glaze.
3 Take the pan from the heat. Whisk in thoroughly 250 g (8 oz) very cold butter, cut into cubes, a few pieces at a time. Move the pan on and off the heat so the butter thickens and becomes creamy without melting to oil.
4 Over high heat bring the sauce just to a boil, whisking. Stir in 30 ml (2 tbsp) chopped mixed fresh herbs, salt, and pepper.
5 Remove the inner leaves and choke from each artichoke as directed. Spoon some sauce into the cup formed by the leaves and serve the rest separately. Decorate with a few herb sprigs.

—— **GETTING AHEAD** ——
The artichokes and red pepper sauce can be made 1 day ahead and kept refrigerated. Reheat both on top of the stove just before serving.

ORIENTAL DEEP-FRIED VEGETABLES

Tempura

🍴 SERVES 6-8 🥄 WORK TIME 45-50 MINUTES ♨ FRYING TIME 3-5 MINUTES

EQUIPMENT

deep-fat fryer

2-pronged fork

small saucepan

deep-fat thermometer (if needed)

baking sheets

grater

chef's knife

small knife

whisk

bowls

vegetable peeler

wide slotted spoon

shallow dishes

sieve

chopping board

paper towels

Tempura was actually introduced into Japan by Portuguese missionaries as a way to cook fish. Today, an authentic version of these Japanese fritters is based on vegetables, though meat, poultry, or shellfish may be added.

INGREDIENTS

water chestnuts

spring onions

eggs

chayotes

broccoli

plain flour

fresh shiitake mushrooms

daikon

mangetout

sweet potatoes

fresh root ginger

oil for deep-frying

sake

light soy sauce

metric	SHOPPING LIST	imperial
1	head of broccoli, weighing about 250 g (8 oz)	1
2	chayotes, total weight about 500 g (1 lb), or 2 courgettes, total weight about 375 g (12 oz)	2
125 g	mangetout	4 oz
8	spring onions	8
2	sweet potatoes, total weight about 300 g (10 oz)	2
250 g	fresh shiitake mushrooms	8 oz
125 g	canned water chestnuts	4 oz
	vegetable oil for deep-frying	
60 g	plain flour for dredging	2 oz
	For the dipping sauce	
60 g	piece of daikon (white radish)	2 oz
2.5 cm	piece of fresh root ginger	1 inch
125 ml	sake	4 fl oz
125 ml	light soy sauce	4 fl oz
	For the batter	
300 g	plain flour	10 oz
2	eggs	2
500 ml	cold water	16 fl oz

ORDER OF WORK

1 **PREPARE THE VEGETABLES**

2 **MAKE THE DIPPING SAUCE**

3 **COAT AND DEEP-FRY THE VEGETABLES**

1 PREPARE THE VEGETABLES

1 Trim the head of broccoli, peeling the stalk with the small knife to remove any tough fibres. Cut the broccoli florets from the stalk where they begin to branch off, leaving about 5 cm (2 inches) of stalk below the floret. Cut large florets in half.

Cut individual florets from broccoli head

Leave piece of stalk on each floret

2 Peel the chayotes with the small knife. Cut in half, cut around and remove the seed, then cut the halves into 5 mm (¼ inch) slices. Or, trim the courgettes and cut them diagonally into 5 mm (¼ inch) slices.

Cut spring onions across into equal length pieces

3 Trim the ends from the mangetout and pull the string down the pod. Repeat at the other end, pulling the string from the other side.

Trim off root ends and thin green tops

4 Trim the spring onions and cut them into 7.5 cm (3 inch) lengths, discarding any thin, dark green ends.

5 Using the vegetable peeler, peel the sweet potatoes, and halve them lengthwise. With the chef's knife, cut the potato halves horizontally into 5 mm (¼ inch) slices.

6 Drain the water chestnuts and slice them thickly with the small knife.

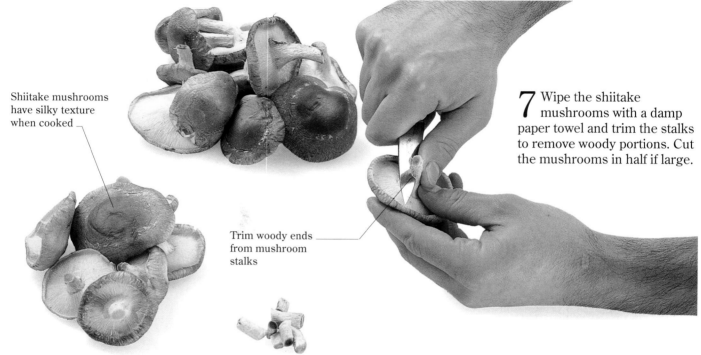

Shiitake mushrooms have silky texture when cooked

Trim woody ends from mushroom stalks

7 Wipe the shiitake mushrooms with a damp paper towel and trim the stalks to remove woody portions. Cut the mushrooms in half if large.

MAKE THE DIPPING SAUCE

1 Trim the end from the piece of daikon, if necessary, then peel it with the vegetable peeler. Grate the daikon.

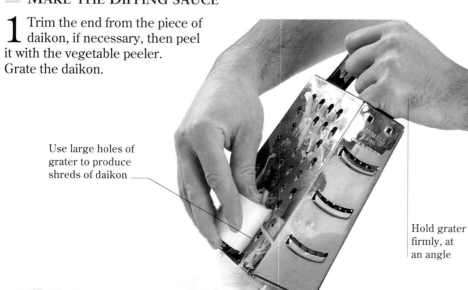

Use large holes of grater to produce shreds of daikon

Hold grater firmly, at an angle

2 With the small knife, cut the skin from the root ginger. With the chef's knife, slice the ginger, cutting across the fibrous grain.

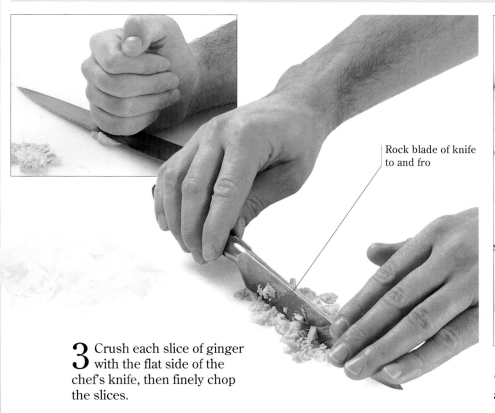

Rock blade of knife
to and fro

3 Crush each slice of ginger with the flat side of the chef's knife, then finely chop the slices.

4 Mix the sake and soy sauce together. Add the grated daikon and chopped ginger and set aside.

3 COAT AND DEEP-FRY THE VEGETABLES

1 To make the batter: lightly beat the eggs in a large bowl. Stir the water into the eggs, using the whisk.

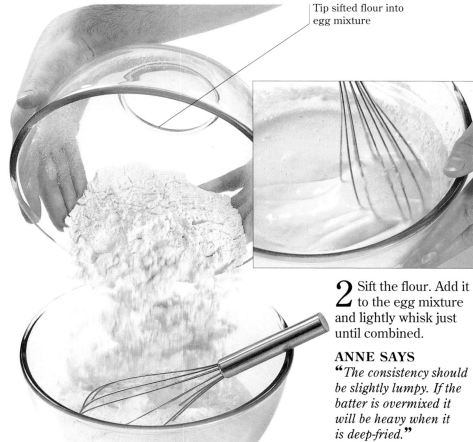

Tip sifted flour into
egg mixture

2 Sift the flour. Add it to the egg mixture and lightly whisk just until combined.

ANNE SAYS
"*The consistency should be slightly lumpy. If the batter is overmixed it will be heavy when it is deep-fried.*"

3 Heat the oil in the deep-fat fryer until it is hot enough to brown a cube of fresh bread in 40 seconds. Heat the oven to very low, for keeping the vegetables warm.

ANNE SAYS
"If using a deep-fat thermometer, it should register 190°C (375°F)."

Toss broccoli in flour so pieces are lightly coated

4 Pour the batter into a large shallow dish. Put the flour for dredging in another shallow dish. Toss the broccoli florets and stalks in the flour to coat lightly.

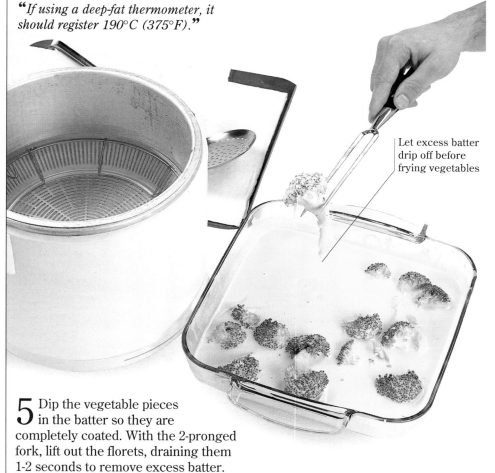

Let excess batter drip off before frying vegetables

5 Dip the vegetable pieces in the batter so they are completely coated. With the 2-pronged fork, lift out the florets, draining them 1-2 seconds to remove excess batter. Lower the pieces gently into the hot oil.

6 Deep-fry the broccoli florets until crisp, 3-5 minutes, turning once during cooking. With the slotted spoon transfer the broccoli to the baking sheet lined with several layers of paper towels. Keep warm.

! TAKE CARE !
It is important to deep-fry in small batches so the fryer is not crowded and the oil temperature remains constant.

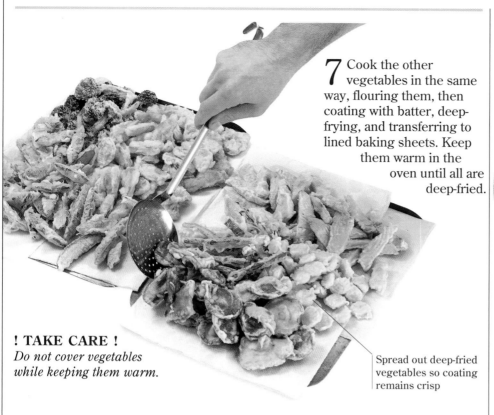

7 Cook the other vegetables in the same way, flouring them, then coating with batter, deep-frying, and transferring to lined baking sheets. Keep them warm in the oven until all are deep-fried.

Spread out deep-fried vegetables so coating remains crisp

! TAKE CARE !
Do not cover vegetables while keeping them warm.

Oriental sauce is pungent and spicy

⚍ TO SERVE
Arrange the deep-fried vegetables on a serving platter. Warm the dipping sauce in the saucepan just until hot, and taste for seasoning. Serve it separately for dipping.

VARIATION
FRITTO MISTO

1 Omit the dipping sauce. Prepare the spring onions and sweet potatoes, as directed in the main recipe.
2 Trim the florets from 1 medium head of cauliflower, cutting large florets in half or into quarters.
3 Prepare 250 g (8 oz) cultivated mushrooms: wipe with a damp paper towel and trim the stalks even with the caps. Cut large caps in half.
4 Peel 250 g (8 oz) asparagus, using the vegetable peeler to strip away the tough outer skin at the bottom of each spear. Cut the spears into 7.5 cm (3 inch) lengths. Blanch in boiling salted water for 3 minutes, drain, rinse with cold water, and drain well again.
5 Cut 250 g (8 oz) mozzarella into sticks about 7.5 cm (3 inches) long. Cut 3-4 lemons into wedges for serving.
6 Lightly flour the vegetables and cheese. Dip the mushrooms and cheese into 2 lightly beaten eggs. Coat with 150 g (5 oz) dried breadcrumbs seasoned with salt and pepper.
7 Deep-fry the coated mushrooms and cheese 3-5 minutes; drain and keep warm. Prepare the batter. Dip the remaining vegetables in batter and deep-fry them as directed.
8 Arrange the cheese and vegetables on individual plates with wedges of lemon for squeezing.

GETTING AHEAD
The vegetables and ingredients for the sauce can be prepared up to 2 hours ahead. Make the batter and deep-fry the vegetables just before serving.

SWISS CHARD CREPES WITH THREE CHEESES

🍽 SERVES 6 🥄 WORK TIME 1 HOUR* 🍲 BAKING TIME 20-25 MINUTES

EQUIPMENT

bowls

vegetable peeler

cheese grater

small knife

chef's knife

plate

small ladle

metal spoon

whisk

palette knife

large frying pan

teaspoon

colander

20 cm (8 inch) crêpe pan**

saucepans

wooden spoon

shallow baking dish

sieve

**flat-bottomed frying pan can also be used

Thin, lacy crêpes are filled with a vigorous combination of Swiss chard, goat cheese, feta, chopped shallots, and garlic, then topped with a light cream sauce. Spinach or pe-tsai (Chinese cabbage) can be substituted for the chard.

* plus 30-60 minutes standing time

metric	SHOPPING LIST	imperial
	butter for baking dish	
	For the crêpe batter	
125 g	plain flour	4 oz
2.5 ml	salt	½ tsp
3	eggs	3
250 ml	milk	8 fl oz
45-60 ml	vegetable oil	3-4 tbsp
	For the Swiss chard and cheese filling	
750 g	Swiss chard	1½ lb
3	shallots	3
2	garlic cloves	2
30 g	butter	1 oz
90 g	soft goat cheese	3 oz
125 g	fresh feta cheese	4 oz
	salt and pepper	
	ground nutmeg	
	For the white cream sauce	
250 ml	milk	8 fl oz
30 g	butter	1 oz
30 ml	plain flour	2 tbsp
125 ml	double cream	4 fl oz
	ground nutmeg	
30 g	Gruyère cheese for sprinkling	1 oz

INGREDIENTS

Swiss chard

garlic cloves

shallots

Gruyère cheese

feta cheese

soft goat cheese

milk

ground nutmeg

eggs

butter

double cream

plain flour

vegetable oil

ORDER OF WORK

1 MAKE THE CREPES

2 PREPARE THE SWISS CHARD

3 MAKE THE FILLING

4 FILL AND BAKE THE CREPES

1 MAKE THE CREPES

1 Sift the flour and salt into a medium bowl and make a well in the centre. Pour the eggs into the well and whisk until just mixed.

2 Add half of the milk and whisk, drawing in the flour to make a paste. Stir in half of the remaining milk. Cover and let stand 30-60 minutes. Meanwhile, prepare the Swiss chard and make the filling (see pages 98-99).

3 After the batter has been standing, stir the remaining milk into the batter, adding enough so it is the consistency of thin cream.

Batter that has been left to stand will make light crêpes, because starch in flour has expanded

Bubbles around edge show crêpe pan is hot

4 To fry the crêpes: heat about 15 ml (1 tbsp) oil in the crêpe pan until very hot; pour off the excess, reserving it to grease the pan later. Add a drop of batter and wait until it sputters, showing the pan is hot. Pour in a small ladle of batter, rotating and shaking the pan so that the batter coats the bottom evenly.

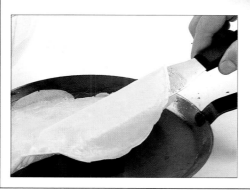

5 Fry the crêpe quickly over medium heat until it is set on top and brown underneath, 1-2 minutes. Loosen the crêpe, then turn or flip it over with the help of the palette knife, and continue cooking the crêpe until it is brown on the other side, 30-60 seconds.

6 Transfer the crêpe to the plate. Continue making crêpes, adding oil to the pan as necessary, until all the batter is used, to make a total of 12 crêpes. Pile them on the plate so that they stay moist and warm.

2 PREPARE THE SWISS CHARD

1 With the chef's knife, trim off the root from the Swiss chard and discard any tough stalks and leaves. Thoroughly wash the stalks and leaves.

2 Cut off the green tops from around the stalks and set the green tops aside. Using the vegetable peeler, remove any strings from the outer sides of the stalks.

Green tops of chard are cooked separately from stalks at this stage

Slice chard stalks in thick chunks

3 Cut the stalks into 1 cm (¹/₂ inch) slices and reserve. Bring a large pan of water to a boil, add salt and the green tops, and simmer until tender, 2-3 minutes. Drain in the colander, rinse with cold water, and drain again thoroughly. Chop the tops with the chef's knife.

3 MAKE THE FILLING

1 Chop the shallots (see box, page 99). Set the flat side of the chef's knife on top of each garlic clove and strike it with your fist. Discard the skin and finely chop the garlic.

Diced shallot adds flavour to filling

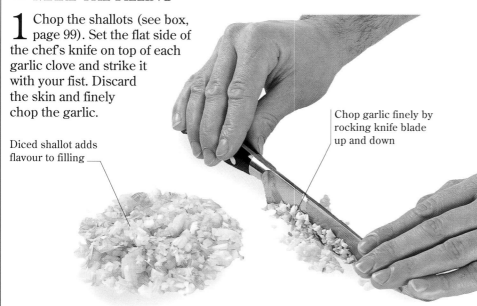

Chop garlic finely by rocking knife blade up and down

2 Heat the butter in the large frying pan. Add the garlic and shallots and cook until soft but not brown, 1-2 minutes. Add the sliced chard stalks and sauté, stirring, until just tender, 3-5 minutes.

Add green chard tops when stalks are tender

3 Add the chopped Swiss chard tops and sauté, stirring, until all moisture has evaporated, 2-3 minutes. Remove the pan from the heat.

4 Crumble the goat cheese into the sautéed Swiss chard mixture, then crumble in the feta cheese. Season to taste with salt, pepper, and a pinch of nutmeg. Stir to mix, then set aside while making the crêpes.

Crumble cheese with fingers

HOW TO CHOP A SHALLOT

For a standard chop, make slices that are about 3 mm (1/8 inch) thick. For a fine chop, make the slices as thin as possible.

1 Peel the outer papery skin from the shallot. Separate into sections at the root, peel section if necessary, and halve. Set each section, flat-side down, on a chopping board, hold steady with your fingers, and slice horizontally, leaving the slices attached at the root end.

2 Slice vertically through the shallot, again leaving the root end uncut.

3 Cut across the shallot to make fine dice. Continue chopping until the dice are very fine.

4 FILL AND BAKE THE CREPES

1 Heat the oven to 180°C (350°F, Gas 4). Butter the baking dish. To make the white cream sauce: scald the milk in a saucepan. Melt the butter in another saucepan over medium heat. Whisk in the flour and cook until foaming, 30-60 seconds.

2 Remove from the heat and let cool slightly, then whisk in the hot milk. Return to the heat and cook, whisking constantly, until the sauce boils and thickens. Whisk in the cream. Season with salt, pepper, and a pinch of nutmeg; simmer 2 minutes. Remove from the heat, cover, and keep warm.

Press cheese against grater with fingertips

3 Grate the Gruyère cheese against the largest holes of the grater.

4 Put 2 spoonfuls of filling onto one half of the paler side of a crêpe.

Baking dish is buttered to keep crêpes from sticking

Attractive brown side of crêpe should be on outside

5 Fold the crêpe in half, then in half again to form a triangle. Arrange the crêpe in the baking dish, then continue filling and folding the crêpes.

6 Repeat until all the crêpes are used, overlapping them in the dish until it is full.

Overlap crêpes to keep them moist

7 If necessary, reheat the sauce, stirring until smooth. Spoon the sauce over the crêpes to coat them completely. Sprinkle with the grated Gruyère cheese. Bake in the heated oven until the sauce is bubbling and brown, 20-25 minutes. Serve hot from the baking dish.

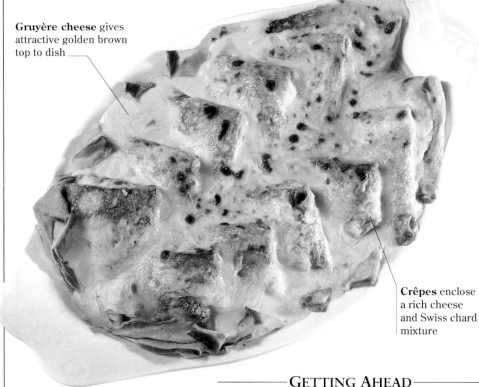

Gruyère cheese gives attractive golden brown top to dish

Crêpes enclose a rich cheese and Swiss chard mixture

GETTING AHEAD
The crêpes can be prepared, filled, and kept up to 3 days in the refrigerator. They can also be frozen. Bake them just before serving.

VARIATION
CREPES WITH WILD MUSHROOMS AND HERBS
Here crêpes are rolled around a juicy filling of wild and button mushrooms.

1 Make the crêpes as directed.
2 Wipe 250 g (8 oz) fresh shiitake or other wild mushrooms with a damp paper towel, trim the stalks, and halve any large mushrooms. Cut into 1 cm (1/2 inch) slices. Or, soak 45 g (1½ oz) dried wild mushrooms in warm water until plump, about 30 minutes, then drain, and continue as for fresh. Clean 250 g (8 oz) button mushrooms, trim the stalks even with the caps, then with stalk-side down, slice.
3 Melt the butter, add the chopped garlic, shallots, and wild and button mushrooms, and sauté until the liquid has evaporated, stirring constantly, about 5 minutes. Set aside a few sautéed mushrooms for garnish.
4 Strip the leaves from several sprigs of fresh herbs such as parsley, tarragon, and chives. Chop the leaves.
5 Make the white sauce as directed, saving the cream to add later, then stir in the herbs. Mix half of the herb sauce with the mushrooms, put mixture in the middle of each crêpe, fold in 2 sides, and roll up into cylinders. Arrange in a buttered baking dish.
6 Add the cream to the remaining herb sauce and pour it over the crêpes. Bake as directed, omitting the grated cheese. Garnish with the reserved mushrooms just before serving.

2 ROAST AND PEEL THE GREEN PEPPERS

Loosened skin peels off easily

1 Heat the grill and set the whole peppers on a rack about 10 cm (4 inches) from the heat. Grill them, turning once or twice, until the skin is black and blistered, 10-12 minutes. Wrap in the plastic bags and let cool.

ANNE SAYS
"The steam trapped inside the plastic bag helps loosen the skin."

2 With the small knife, peel off the skin from each pepper, then rinse the peeled peppers under cold running water. Pat them dry with paper towels.

3 Cut out the core from the centre of each pepper, then scrape out the seeds with the teaspoon and discard them.

3 STUFF THE GREEN PEPPERS

Pack stuffing into peppers

1 Chop the onions. Heat the vegetable oil in the frying pan, add the onions, and cook, stirring, until soft but not brown. Let cool. Grate the cheese and put it in a bowl. Add the oregano, salt, pepper, and sautéed onions and mix well together. Taste the stuffing for seasoning.

2 Oil the baking dish. Spoon the cheese-onion mixture into each prepared pepper and put the peppers sideways in the dish.

ANNE SAYS
"The stuffed peppers should fit snugly in the baking dish."

4 BAKE THE GREEN PEPPERS

1 Heat the oven to 180°C (350°F, Gas 4). Make the custard: whisk together the eggs, milk, oregano, salt, and pepper. Pour the custard around the peppers.

Pour herbed custard into baking dish

Peppers are plump when filled

2 Bake in the heated oven for 45-50 minutes; test whether the custard is set with the point of a knife.

🍽 TO SERVE
Decorate the tomato salsa with fresh coriander leaves and serve with the hot stuffed peppers.

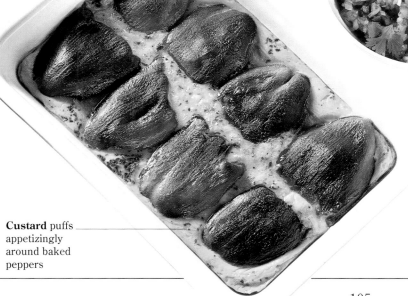

Custard puffs appetizingly around baked peppers

Piquant salsa makes good accompaniment to baked peppers

V A R I A T I O N

RED PEPPERS STUFFED WITH SWEETCORN

Red peppers, stuffed with sweetcorn and cheese, make a pretty presentation.

1 Cook 2 corn cobs in a large pan of boiling water until the kernels pop out easily when tested with the point of a knife, 15-20 minutes. Drain the corn and cut the corn kernels from the cob. Alternatively, thaw 150 g (5 oz) frozen sweetcorn kernels, or use an equal amount of drained canned sweetcorn.
2 Make the tomato salsa as directed.
3 Peel, core, and deseed 8 red peppers as directed.
4 Make the cheese filling as directed and stir in the sweetcorn. Stuff the peppers and arrange upright in individual baking dishes, 2 peppers to each dish.
5 Pour in the custard and bake as directed.

GETTING AHEAD
The peppers can be stuffed and the tomato salsa made up to 24 hours ahead and refrigerated. Make the custard and bake the peppers just before serving.

STIR-FRIED THAI VEGETABLES

🍽 SERVES 4   🥣 WORK TIME 30-35 MINUTES   ♨ BAKING TIME 15-20 MINUTES

EQUIPMENT

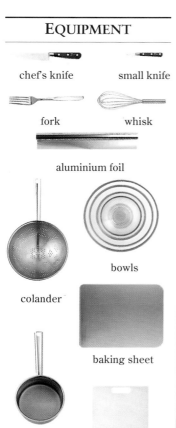

chef's knife   small knife

fork   whisk

aluminium foil

colander

bowls

baking sheet

large saucepan

chopping board

pastry brush

baking dish

wok with stirrer*

*large frying pan can also be used

Almost any crisp vegetable is excellent stir-fried; this cooking method keeps the textures of the vegetables firm and the colours vivid.

GETTING AHEAD
Last-minute cooking is essential for a stir-fry. However, the vegetables can be prepared up to 2 hours ahead. The rice can also be cooked ahead and reheated in a low oven.

metric	SHOPPING LIST	imperial
300 g	long-grain rice	10 oz
	salt	
30 g	dried oriental mushrooms, or other dried wild mushrooms	1 oz
250 ml	warm water, more if needed	8 fl oz
60 g	skinned unsalted peanuts	2 oz
	butter for dish and foil	
1	cauliflower, weighing about 500 g (1 lb)	1
500 g	bok choy	1 lb
175 g	mangetout	6 oz
2	garlic cloves	2
1	medium red pepper	1
3-5	sprigs of fresh basil	3-5
175 g	bean sprouts	6 oz
1	stalk of lemon grass or 1 lemon	1
45 ml	fish sauce (nam pla)	3 tbsp
30 ml	oyster sauce	2 tbsp
5 ml	cornflour	1 tsp
5 ml	sugar	1 tsp
45 ml	vegetable oil	3 tbsp
2	dried red chillies	2

INGREDIENTS

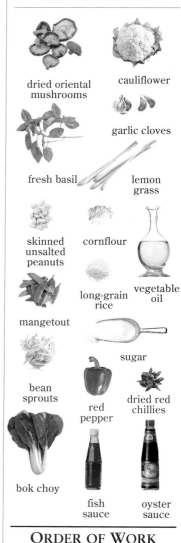

dried oriental mushrooms

cauliflower

garlic cloves

fresh basil   lemon grass

skinned unsalted peanuts

cornflour

vegetable oil

long-grain rice

mangetout

sugar

bean sprouts

red pepper

dried red chillies

bok choy

fish sauce

oyster sauce

ORDER OF WORK

1   **BOIL THE RICE**

2   **PREPARE THE VEGETABLES**

3   **STIR-FRY THE VEGETABLES**

1 BOIL THE RICE

1 Cook the long-grain rice in boiling salted water until barely tender, 10-12 minutes. Meanwhile, soak the dried mushrooms and toast the peanuts (see Prepare the Vegetables, steps 1 and 2, below).

2 Drain the rice in the colander, rinse with cold running water to wash away the starch, and let drain thoroughly. Using the pastry brush, butter the baking dish and enough foil to cover the dish.

3 Spread the cooked rice evenly in the buttered baking dish, using the fork to fluff up the grains, and cover the dish with the buttered foil. Keep warm in the oven, turned to its lowest setting, after toasting the peanuts.

2 PREPARE THE VEGETABLES

1 Heat the oven to 190°C (375°F, Gas 5). Put the dried mushrooms in a bowl, pour over warm water to cover, and set the mushrooms aside to soften, about 30 minutes.

2 Meanwhile, spread the peanuts on the baking sheet and toast them in the oven until brown, 5-7 minutes. Coarsely chop them.

3 Trim the cauliflower to remove the outer green leaves. With the small knife, cut off the florets, discarding the stalks.

4 Trim the stalks of the bok choy. Cut each head lengthwise in half. Pile the halves 2-3 at a time on the chopping board and slice them crosswise into shreds.

Hold bok choy firmly when slicing

5 Trim the ends from the mangetout and pull the string down the pod. Repeat at the other end, pulling the string from the other side.

6 Drain the mushrooms and slice them. Set the flat side of the chef's knife on top of the garlic cloves and strike it with your fist. Skin and finely chop the garlic cloves.

Rinse bean sprouts with cold water

7 With a sharp movement, twist the core out of the pepper, then halve the pepper and scrape out the seeds. Cut away the white ribs on the inside. Set each pepper half on the chopping board, flatten it, and slice it lengthwise into strips. Remove the basil leaves from the stalks.

8 Rinse the bean sprouts in the colander. Trim the lemon grass. Slice the stalk lengthwise in half if it is large, then cut across to chop it. Alternatively, grate the zest from the lemon.

3 STIR-FRY THE VEGETABLES

1 Put the fish sauce, oyster sauce, cornflour, sugar, and chopped lemon grass in a small bowl, and whisk them together.

2 Heat the oil in the wok. Add the chopped garlic and dried red chillies and stir-fry until the garlic is fragrant, 30 seconds. Add the cauliflower, red pepper, bean sprouts, and bok choy and cook, stirring constantly, until beginning to soften, 3-5 minutes.

Bok choy will wilt and lose volume

Lift and turn vegetables as they fry

3 Stir the mushrooms and mangetout into the vegetables in the wok and cook, stirring, 3 minutes.

4 Add the basil leaves and fish sauce mixture to the vegetables in the wok, and stir-fry 2 minutes longer. Taste and season with more fish sauce, oyster sauce, and sugar, if needed. Remove the chillies and discard.

ANNE SAYS
"As the mixture cooks, the cornflour will slightly thicken the sauce."

¶❂¶ TO SERVE
Make a ring of rice on a warmed plate. Spoon the vegetables and sauce into the centre, and sprinkle with the chopped peanuts. If you like, pull out a few red pepper strips and arrange them decoratively on the rice.

Chopped toasted peanuts give crunchy texture

Red pepper strips are bright garnish on rice

VARIATION
CHINESE STIR-FRIED VEGETABLES
This vegetable stir-fry is best served with boiled Chinese noodles.

1 Prepare the oriental mushrooms, bok choy, and bean sprouts as directed; omit the cauliflower, mangetout, and red pepper.
2 Omit the peanuts; toast 45 g (1½ oz) flaked almonds in the oven, 3-5 minutes.
3 Trim 1 medium head of broccoli, leaving about 5 cm (2 inches) of the stalk. Strip the tough outer skin from the stalk. Cut off the florets and cut the stalk into 7.5 cm (3 inch) sticks.
4 Drain 60 g (2 oz) canned bamboo shoots and 60 g (2 oz) canned baby corn. Slice the green parts of 2 spring onions.
5 Omit the fish sauce mixture. Whisk together 45 ml (3 tbsp) rice wine or dry sherry, 30 ml (2 tbsp) soy sauce, 10 ml (2 tsp) sesame oil, 5 ml (1 tsp) cornflour, and a pinch of sugar.
6 Heat the oil in the wok, add the broccoli and bok choy, and stir-fry 2-3 minutes. Add the mushrooms and baby corn and stir-fry 2 minutes.
7 Add the soy sauce mixture, bamboo shoots, bean sprouts, and spring onions, and cook, stirring, 2 minutes. Season with more rice wine, soy sauce, sesame oil, and sugar, if needed, and sprinkle with the toasted flaked almonds.

MIXED VEGETABLE CURRY

Sabzi Kari

🍽 SERVES 6-8   🥣 WORK TIME 45-50 MINUTES   🍲 COOKING TIME 25-35 MINUTES

EQUIPMENT

saucepans, 1 with lid

mortar and pestle*

bowls

colander

small frying pan

small knife

chef's knife

chopping board

wooden spoon

sieve

slotted spoon

large metal spoon

thin tea towel**

sauté pan with lid***

vegetable peeler

kitchen fork

*spice mill can also be used
**muslin can also be used
***frying pan with lid can also be used

INGREDIENTS

basmati rice

dried red chillies

cinnamon stick

seeds

ground spices

cardamom pods

cloves

potatoes

vegetable oil

carrots

cauliflower

peas

onions

garlic cloves

French beans

desiccated coconut

tomatoes

This vegetable curry is flavoured with an exotic blend of spices and served with basmati rice. Chutney and a "raita" of diced cucumber and plain yogurt are also excellent accompaniments.

metric	SHOPPING LIST	imperial
400 g	basmati rice	13 oz
150 g	desiccated coconut	5 oz
	salt	
	For the curry spice mixture	
6	dried red chillies	6
12	cardamom pods	12
45 ml	coriander seeds	3 tbsp
15 ml	cumin seeds	1 tbsp
2.5 ml	mustard seeds	½ tsp
10 ml each	fenugreek seeds, ground turmeric, and ground ginger	2 tsp each
	For the vegetable stew	
3	garlic cloves	3
4 each	medium onions, potatoes, and carrots, total weight about 1.25 kg (2¾ lb)	4 each
1	cauliflower, weighing about 1 kg (2 lb)	1
500 g	French beans	1 lb
4	large tomatoes, total weight about 750 g (1½ lb)	4
75 ml	vegetable oil	2½ fl oz
1	cinnamon stick	1
6	whole cloves	6
250 g	shelled fresh or defrosted peas	8 oz

ORDER OF WORK

1 MAKE THE CURRY SPICE MIXTURE

2 PREPARE THE COCONUT MILK AND VEGETABLES

3 MAKE THE VEGETABLE CURRY

4 COOK THE BASMATI RICE

1 MAKE THE CURRY SPICE MIXTURE

1 Split the dried red chillies and discard the seeds.

Scrape out seeds with small knife

2 Crush the cardamom pods in the mortar with the pestle and discard the pods, keeping the cardamom seeds in the mortar.

ANNE SAYS
"You can also use the end of a rolling pin to crush the cardamom pods."

3 Put the chillies in the small frying pan with the coriander seeds and cumin seeds and toast the spices over medium heat, stirring constantly to prevent burning, until they are browned and very fragrant, about 2 minutes. Set aside to cool.

ANNE SAYS
"For toasting the spices, the pan should be dry, with no fat."

4 Put the toasted spices in the mortar with the cardamom seeds and add the mustard seeds and fenugreek seeds. Crush them to a fine powder.

ANNE SAYS
"The curry spice mixture can be kept up to a month in an airtight jar."

Ready ground spices are added to those prepared by hand

5 Add the turmeric and ginger, and stir the spices well to mix.

HOW TO MAKE COCONUT MILK

Not the same as the liquid inside a coconut, coconut "milk" is made by steeping desiccated coconut in water.

1 Bring 750 ml (1¼ pints) water to a boil in a small saucepan. Add the desiccated coconut and stir with the wooden spoon to mix, then cover and remove from heat. Let stand about 30 minutes.

Here, muslin is used to catch coconut and allows only liquid to drain through

Coconut has absorbed most of water

2 Put a tea towel or piece of muslin in a sieve set in a bowl and pour in the coconut and its liquid.

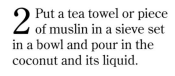

3 Gather up the ends of the cloth and squeeze the desiccated coconut well to extract as much liquid or "milk" as possible. Discard the desiccated coconut.

2 PREPARE THE COCONUT MILK AND VEGETABLES

1 Make coconut milk with 750 ml (1¼ pints) water and the coconut (see box, left). Set the flat side of the chef's knife on top of each garlic clove and strike it with your fist. Discard the skin and finely chop the garlic.

2 Peel the onions, leaving a little of the roots attached, and cut in half. Slice each half horizontally towards the root, then slice vertically, again leaving the root end uncut. Finally, cut across the onion to make dice.

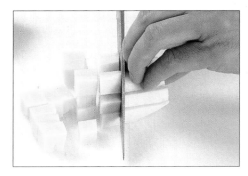

3 Peel the potatoes and square off the sides. Cut each one vertically into 1 cm (½ inch) slices, then stack the slices and cut into 1 cm (½ inch) strips. Cut across to make 1 cm (½ inch) dice. Put in a bowl of water.

4 Trim the florets from the cauliflower stalk and leaves. Cut the florets into small pieces.

Cauliflower florets need not be cut in even-sized pieces

Florets make crunchy curry ingredient

5 Peel the carrots, then roll-cut them: cut a diagonal slice near the end of 1 carrot. Turn the carrot a quarter turn and make another diagonal cut in it. Continue to turn and cut all the carrot; repeat with the remaining carrots.

6 Snap off the ends of the beans and cut them into 5 cm (2 inch) pieces.

7 Score an "x" on the base of each tomato. Immerse in boiling water until the skin starts to split, 8-15 seconds. Transfer to a bowl of cold water. When cold, peel off the skin.

Discard seeds to leave tomato flesh

8 Cut the tomatoes in half and squeeze out the seeds. Cut each half into quarters.

3 MAKE THE VEGETABLE CURRY

1 Heat the oil in the sauté pan, add the cinnamon stick and cloves, and cook until fragrant, 30-60 seconds.

2 Add the onions and garlic to the spices in the pan and sauté quickly, stirring to soften and cook evenly, until just beginning to colour.

3 Add the curry spice mixture and cook over low heat, stirring constantly, about 2-3 minutes.

Fresh or frozen peas are good in curry

Each vegetable adds different texture

4 Drain the potatoes and add to the pan with the carrots, cauliflower, French beans, tomatoes, peas, and salt to taste. Sauté, stirring occasionally, until thoroughly coated with spices, 3-5 minutes.

5 Add the coconut milk to the vegetables and stir together. Cover the pan and simmer until the vegetables are tender and the sauce is thick and rich, 15-20 minutes. Meanwhile, cook the basmati rice.

Coconut milk adds exotic flavour

Spices coat vegetables and give delicious aroma

6 Remove the cloves and cinnamon stick from the pan and discard. Taste the curry for seasoning.

4 COOK THE BASMATI RICE

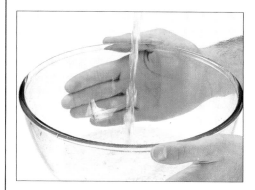

1 Put the basmati rice in a large bowl, cover generously with cold water, and let soak 2-3 minutes, stirring occasionally. Drain the rice in the colander, rinse with cold water, and drain again thoroughly.

2 Put the drained rice in a saucepan with 850 ml (scant 1½ pints) water and a pinch of salt. Bring to a boil, then cover the pan and simmer until the rice is just tender to the bite (al dente), 10-12 minutes. Remove from heat and leave covered for at least 5 minutes, then gently stir the rice to fluff it.

ANNE SAYS
"Do not remove the lid until just before serving, so that the rice will remain warm and fluffy."

🍽 TO SERVE
Divide the rice among warmed plates, spoon the vegetable curry next to it, and serve hot.

Vegetables and rice make dramatic presentation when served in this way

VARIATION

WINTER VEGETABLE CURRY

Mixed Vegetable Curry takes a seasonal turn with a selection of winter vegetables.

1 Prepare the curry spice mixture, coconut milk, onions, garlic, potatoes, carrots, and cauliflower as directed in the main recipe; omit the green beans, tomatoes, and peas.
2 Discard the seeds from a 500 g (1 lb) piece of pumpkin, cut it into 7.5 cm (3 inch) pieces, and peel them with a small knife. Dice the flesh.
3 Trim, peel, and dice 3 turnips (total weight about 375 g/12 oz). Trim 250 g (8 oz) Brussels sprouts.
4 Sauté the onions and garlic with the curry spice mixture. Add the prepared vegetables and continue with the curry as directed in the main recipe, simmering it 15-20 minutes.
5 Spread the rice in a large, shallow serving bowl. Spoon out a few of the Brussels sprouts to arrange on the rice. Mould the curry in a bowl: oil a deep soup bowl, fill it with curry, and press down lightly. Leave 1 minute, then turn out onto the rice. For a quicker serving, make a well in the centre and add the vegetable curry. Serve hot.

GETTING AHEAD
The vegetable curry can be made up to 3 days in advance and refrigerated.

AUBERGINE CANNELLONI

|O| SERVES 4-6   ☙ WORK TIME 40-45 MINUTES   ♨ COOKING TIME 50-60 MINUTES

EQUIPMENT

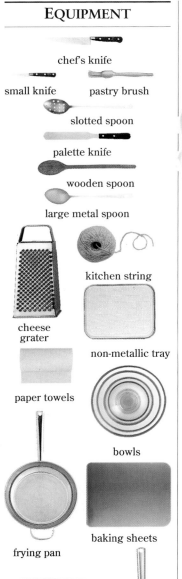

chef's knife

small knife   pastry brush

slotted spoon

palette knife

wooden spoon

large metal spoon

kitchen string

cheese grater

non-metallic tray

paper towels

bowls

frying pan

baking sheets

large baking dish   saucepan

chopping board

Thin slices of lightly baked aubergine are wrapped around ricotta and mozzarella cheeses, flavoured with basil. Baked in a thick tomato sauce with a sprinkling of Parmesan cheese, they resemble filled pasta cannelloni. Choose broad aubergines that will provide wide slices for filling.

GETTING AHEAD

The "cannelloni" can be baked 2 days ahead. Cover and chill. Reheat 15-20 minutes at 180°C (350°F, Gas 4).

* plus 30 minutes standing time

metric	SHOPPING LIST	imperial
4	aubergines, total weight about 1.4 kg (3 lb)	4
	salt and pepper	
60 ml	olive oil	4 tbsp
250 g	mozzarella cheese	8 oz
1	medium bunch of fresh basil	1
250 g	ricotta cheese	8 oz
30 g	grated Parmesan cheese	1 oz
	For the tomato sauce	
1.4 kg	medium tomatoes	3 lb
5	garlic cloves	5
3	medium onions	3
75 ml	olive oil	2½ fl oz
90 ml	tomato purée	3 fl oz
1	bouquet garni (see box, page 118)	1
	granulated sugar	

INGREDIENTS

aubergines

bouquet garni   garlic cloves

fresh basil

tomato purée   tomatoes

olive oil   grated Parmesan cheese

granulated sugar   onions

mozzarella cheese   ricotta cheese

ORDER OF WORK

1 **PREPARE THE AUBERGINES**

2 **MAKE THE TOMATO SAUCE**

3 **FILL AND BAKE THE AUBERGINE CANNELLONI**

1 PREPARE THE AUBERGINES

1 Trim the aubergines and cut them lengthwise into 1 cm (½ inch) slices. Lay the slices on the non-metallic tray, in one layer, and sprinkle them generously on both sides with salt. Leave 30 minutes. Heat the oven to 190°C (375°F, Gas 5).

ANNE SAYS
"Salting aubergine slices draws out the bitter juices."

Chef's knife cuts cleanly through aubergine

2 Rinse the aubergine slices with cold water and dry them on paper towels. Lightly brush one side of each slice with olive oil and set slices oil-side down on the baking sheets. Brush the tops with more oil.

Brush on oil lightly because aubergine will absorb it all

3 Bake the aubergine slices, turning them once, until tender and lightly browned, about 20 minutes. Meanwhile, make the tomato sauce. Let the slices cool on the baking sheets. Leave the oven heated.

! TAKE CARE !
Bake aubergine slices until just tender, otherwise they will be too soft to handle.

2 MAKE THE TOMATO SAUCE

1 Score an "x" on the base of each tomato. Immerse in boiling water until the skin starts to split. Transfer to cold water, then peel. Halve the tomatoes, squeeze out seeds, and chop.

After blanching, skins will slip off easily

2 Strike flat side of the chef's knife on each garlic clove. Peel garlic and finely chop. Peel onions, leaving a little root attached, and cut in half. Slice each half horizontally, leaving attached at root end, then slice vertically, again leaving root end uncut. Cut across to make dice. Chop dice until very fine.

3 Heat the oil in the frying pan, add the diced onions, and cook over medium heat, stirring occasionally with the wooden spoon, until soft but not brown, 3-4 minutes. Add the garlic, tomato purée, bouquet garni, chopped tomatoes, a pinch of sugar, salt, and pepper. Cover and cook over very low heat about 10 minutes.

4 Uncover the frying pan and continue cooking the tomato sauce, stirring occasionally, until it is thick, about 15 minutes longer. Lift out the bouquet garni with the wooden spoon and discard it. Taste the sauce for seasoning and adjust if necessary.

This package of flavouring herbs is designed to be easily lifted from the pot and discarded at the end of cooking. To make, hold 2-3 sprigs of fresh thyme, 1 bay leaf, and 10-12 parsley stalks together. Wind a piece of string around the herbs and tie, leaving a length to tie to the pot handle if necessary.

3 FILL AND BAKE THE AUBERGINE CANNELLONI

1 Spread one-third of the tomato sauce in the bottom of a baking dish, about 23 x 32 cm (9 x 13 inches).

2 Cut the mozzarella into 1 cm (1/2 inch) slices, and then into 1 cm (1/2 inch) sticks. Pull the basil leaves from the stalks, reserving a few basil sprigs for garnish.

ANNE SAYS
"You will need a basil leaf for each slice of aubergine."

Put mozzarella at narrow end ready to roll up aubergine

3 Using the palette knife, spread a slice of aubergine with 15 ml (1 tbsp) ricotta cheese. Put a basil leaf at one end, set a mozzarella stick on top, and sprinkle with pepper. Roll up the aubergine slice. Trim mozzarella if necessary.

4 Transfer the roll to the baking dish and repeat with the remaining aubergine slices, ricotta, basil, and mozzarella cheese, filling the dish with the "cannelloni".

5 Spoon the remaining tomato sauce over the "cannelloni" and sprinkle with the grated Parmesan cheese. Bake in the oven until very hot and bubbling, 20-25 minutes.

Spoon on tomato sauce to cover cannelloni evenly

🍴 TO SERVE
Transfer servings of aubergine "cannelloni" to individual warmed plates, spoon some of the tomato sauce on top, and decorate with the reserved basil sprigs.

Aubergine cannelloni is rich and juicy

V A R I A T I O N
AUBERGINE FEUILLES

1 Trim the aubergines and cut them crosswise into 1 cm (1/2 inch) rounds. There should be 36 rounds (6 per person). Spread them on a large non-metallic tray, sprinkle with salt, and leave 20-30 minutes; then rinse, dry, and bake with olive oil as directed.
2 Make the tomato sauce as directed, cooking 5-10 minutes longer to remove extra moisture. Let it cool to tepid.
3 Cut 300 g (10 oz) mozzarella cheese into 24 slices 5 mm (1/4 inch) wide.
4 Stir the ricotta cheese into half of the cooled tomato sauce and taste for seasoning.
5 Pull the basil leaves from the stalks, saving 6 sprigs for garnish.
6 Oil a baking sheet. Spread a large aubergine round with about 30-45 ml (2-3 tbsp) of the tomato and cheese filling, top with a slice of mozzarella and 2-3 basil leaves, then add another round of aubergine, smaller than the first. Repeat with another layer of the filling, cheese, and basil, and finish with a small round of aubergine. Secure the "feuilles" with a wooden cocktail stick so they hold together during baking.
7 Transfer to the baking sheet and continue with the remaining aubergine rounds and filling.
8 Bake the "feuilles" in the heated oven just until very hot and the mozzarella has melted, 10-15 minutes.
9 Reheat the remaining sauce. Spoon onto warmed plates and set the hot "feuilles" on top. Remove the cocktail sticks; decorate with sprigs of basil.

SUMMER FRITTATA WITH RATATOUILLE

IOI SERVES 3-4   WORK TIME 20-25 MINUTES   COOKING TIME 20-25 MINUTES

EQUIPMENT

whisk

slotted spoon

chef's knife

fork

small knife

kitchen scissors

string

paper towels

bowls

saucepan

colander

tray

25 cm (10 inch)
frying pan with lid**

chopping board

**omelette pan can also be used

Frittata is an Italian-style omelette. The flavouring here is a ratatouille of summer vegetables, but any chopped leftover vegetable can be substituted – and while the eggs cook slowly, you can sit back and enjoy a glass of wine.

GETTING AHEAD

The ratatouille filling can be prepared up to 24 hours ahead and refrigerated. Cook the frittata just before serving.

* plus standing and cooling time

metric	SHOPPING LIST	imperial
6	eggs	6
	salt and pepper	
15-30 g	butter	1/2-1 oz
	For the ratatouille filling	
1	large bouquet garni (10-12 parsley stalks, 4-5 fresh thyme sprigs, and 2 bay leaves)	1
1	small aubergine, weighing about 250 g (8 oz)	1
1	medium courgette, weighing about 125 g (4 oz)	1
2	garlic cloves	2
1	medium onion	1
250 g	tomatoes	8 oz
1	medium green pepper	1
5-7	sprigs of fresh thyme	5-7
60 ml	olive oil, more if needed	4 tbsp
2.5 ml	ground coriander	1/2 tsp

INGREDIENTS

tomatoes

green pepper

onion

olive oil

butter

eggs

courgette

aubergine

fresh thyme

bouquet garni

ground coriander

garlic cloves

ORDER OF WORK

1 PREPARE THE RATATOUILLE FILLING

2 COOK THE RATATOUILLE FILLING

3 COOK THE FRITTATA

120

PREPARE THE RATATOUILLE FILLING

1 Tie together herbs for bouquet garni with string. Trim the aubergine and cut it lengthwise in half. Cut each half into 4-5 lengthwise strips; cut the strips across into 1 cm (½ inch) chunks.

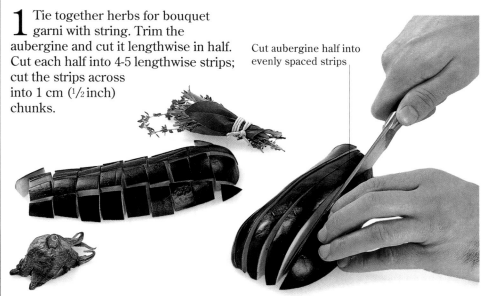

Cut aubergine half into evenly spaced strips

2 Trim the courgette and cut it lengthwise in half. Cut each half crosswise into 1 cm (½ inch) slices.

3 Put the aubergine and courgette on the tray and sprinkle generously with salt. Leave 30 minutes to draw out the bitter juices. Transfer to the colander, rinse with cold water, and pat dry with paper towels.

6 Cut the cores from the tomatoes and score an "x" on the base of each with the tip of a knife. Immerse them in boiling water until the skin splits, 8-15 seconds depending on their ripeness. Transfer them at once to a bowl of cold water. When cold, peel off the skin.

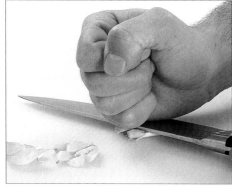

4 Strike the flat side of the chef's knife on each garlic clove with your fist. Skin and finely chop the cloves.

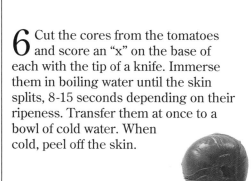

Use small knife to pull skin from tomatoes

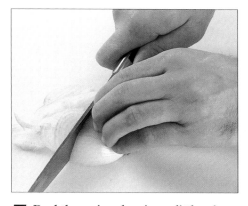

5 Peel the onion, leaving a little of the root attached, and cut it in half through the root and stalk. Lay each onion half flat on the chopping board and cut vertically into thin slices.

ANNE SAYS
"The root holds the onion together."

7 Cut the tomatoes crosswise in half, squeeze out the seeds and discard. Chop each half.

8 With a sharp movement, twist the core out of the green pepper, then halve the pepper and scrape out the seeds. Cut away the white ribs on the inside. Set each pepper half cut-side down on the board and slice it lengthwise into strips.

Lay pepper skin-side up when slicing

9 Strip the thyme leaves from the stalks, reserving a few small sprigs for decoration, and pile the leaves on the chopping board. With the chef's knife, finely chop the leaves.

2 COOK THE RATATOUILLE FILLING

1 Heat about half of the oil in the frying pan. Add the aubergine pieces to the pan and stir-fry until browned, 3-5 minutes. Transfer to a bowl with the slotted spoon.

2 Put the courgette in the pan and stir-fry, adding more oil if necessary, until browned, about 3 minutes. Transfer to the bowl and set aside with the aubergine.

3 Add the green pepper strips to the pan with a little more oil and stir-fry until limp; remove the strips to the bowl. Heat about 15 ml (1 tbsp) more oil in the pan, add the onion, and sauté until lightly browned, 2-3 minutes.

Crisp strips of green pepper will soften as they fry

4 Return the aubergine, courgette, and green pepper to the pan and add the tomatoes, garlic, salt, pepper, chopped thyme, coriander, and the bouquet garni. Stir until mixed. Cover and cook until all the vegetables are tender, 10-15 minutes. Discard the bouquet garni. Let cool completely.

3 COOK THE FRITTATA

1 Whisk the eggs in a bowl until completely mixed. Stir in the ratatouille mixture and season with salt and pepper.

2 Wipe the frying pan; melt the butter over medium heat until foaming, then add the egg mixture.

3 Reduce the heat, cover with the lid, and cook very gently until the centre of the frittata is set, and the base is cooked and lightly browned when you lift the edge with the fork, 20-25 minutes.

Lift edge of frittata gently to check if it is cooked

Fresh thyme sprigs
mirror herb flavouring of omelette

🍽 **TO SERVE**
Invert the frittata onto a large warmed plate and decorate with the reserved thyme sprigs. Cut the frittata into wedges for serving.

SWEETCORN, SPRING ONION, AND RED PEPPER FRITTATA

The yellow, green, and red of the vegetables make a colourful alternative filling.

1 Cook 3 corn cobs in a large pan of boiling water until the kernels pop out easily when tested with the point of a knife, 15-20 minutes. Drain and cut the kernels from the cob. Alternatively, defrost 210 g (7 oz) frozen kernels.
2 Slice 4 spring onions. Core, deseed, and slice 1 medium red pepper.
3 Peel and dice 2 potatoes (total weight about 250 g/8 oz). Put them in a pan of water, add salt, bring to a boil, and simmer until tender, 6-8 minutes. Drain thoroughly.
4 Whisk the eggs in a bowl until well mixed and stir in the corn kernels, spring onions, red pepper, and potato. Season with salt and pepper.
5 Cook the frittata as directed in the main recipe. Run a knife around the edge of the frittata to loosen it, and slide it onto a warmed plate for serving.

INDEX

3346733

ACKNOWLEDGEMENTS

Photographers David Murray
Jules Selmes
Assisted by Ian Boddy

Chef Eric Treuille
Cookery Consultant Linda Collister
Assisted by Joanna Pitchfork

Typesetting Rowena Feeny
Deborah Rhodes
Text film by Disc to Print (UK) Limited

Production Consultant Lorraine Baird

*Carroll & Brown Limited
would like to thank ICTC
(081 568-4179) for supplying the
Cuisinox Elysee pans used throughout the
book, and Moulinex Swan Holdings
Limited for the deep-fat fryer.*

*Anne Willan would like to thank
her chief editor Cynthia Nims and
associate editor Kate Krader for their
vital help with writing the book and
researching and testing the recipes,
aided by La Varenne's chefs
and trainees.*

NOTES

- Metric and imperial measures have
  been calculated separately. Only use
  one set of measures as they are not
  exact equivalents.

- All spoon measurements are level.

- Spoon measurements are calculated
  using a standard 5 ml teaspoon and
  15 ml tablespoon to give an accurate
  measurement of small amounts.